Fodor's POCKET

honolulu
and waikīkī

third edition

Excerpted from *Fodor's Hawai'i*

fodor's travel publications
new york • toronto • london • sydney • auckland
www.fodors.com

contents

maps

on the road with fodor's

A TRIP TAKES YOU OUT OF YOURSELF. Concerns of life at home disappear, driven away by more immediate thoughts—about, say, what marvels will beguile the next day, or where you'll have dinner. That's where Fodor's comes in. We make sure that you know all your options in Honolulu, so that you don't miss something that's around the next bend just because you didn't know it was there. Mindful that the best memories of your trip might have nothing to do with what you came to see, we guide you to sights large and small. With Fodor's at your side, serendipitous discoveries are never far away.

Our success in showing you every corner of Honolulu is a credit to our extraordinary writers. They're the kind of people you'd poll for travel advice if you knew them.

Geographer, photographer, writer, and chef **Daniel Taras** has crisscrossed the globe with extended layovers in Hawai'i, where he once owned and operated his own café and sushi bar in Upcountry Maui. He updated Practical Information.

Maggie Wunsch felt the lure of Hawai'i during her first visit to O'ahu as a child. She returned to the island when she started college and has been there ever since. A freelance journalist, Maggie's travelogues, stories, and writings about Hawai'i's people, places, and events can be found on radio, television, in print, and on the Internet.

Don't Forget to Write

Your experiences—positive and negative—matter to us. If we have missed or misstated something, we want to hear about it. We follow up on all suggestions. Contact the Pocket Honolulu editor at editors@fodors.com or c/o Fodor's at 1745 Broadway, New York, NY, 10019. And have a fabulous trip!

Karen Cure

Editorial Director

honolulu
and waikīkī

In This Chapter

Updated by Maggie Wunsch

introducing honolulu and waikīkī

FOR THOSE WHO LOVE the sophistication of the city but yearn for the pleasures of nature's most abundant beauty, O'ahu is an island to return to again and again. Part of its dramatic appearance lies in its majestic highlands: the western Wai'anae Mountains rise 4,000 ft above sea level, and the verdant Ko'olau Mountains cross the island's midsection at elevations of more than 3,000 ft. Eons of wind and weather erosion have carved these ranges' sculptured, jagged peaks, deep valleys, sheer green cliffs, and dynamic vistas. At the base of these mountains more than 50 beach parks lie draped like a beautiful lei, each known for a different activity, be it snorkeling, surfing, swimming, or sunbathing.

Third-largest of the Hawaiian Islands and covering 608 square mi, O'ahu was formed by two volcanoes that erupted 4 to 6 million years ago. Honolulu, the nation's 11th-largest city, is here, and 75% of Hawai'i's 1.1 million residents call the island home. Somehow, amid all this urban development, you are never more than a glimpse away from a breathtaking ocean or mountain view.

Hawai'i's last kings and queens ruled from 'Iolani Palace in downtown Honolulu. Today, 'Iolani stands as an elegant tribute to Hawai'i's rich history as a kingdom, republic, territory, and state. Even in the days of royalty, the virtues of Waikīkī as a vacation destination were recognized. Long processions of *ali'i* (nobility) made their way across streams and swamps, past the duck ponds, to the coconut groves and the beach.

By the 1880s guest houses were scattered along the south shore like so many seashells. The first hotel, the Moana (now the Sheraton Moana Surfrider), was built at the turn of the 20th century and christened "The First Lady of Waikīkī." The Moana's inaugural room rates of $1.50 per night were the talk of the town. In 1927 the "Pink Palace of the Pacific," the Royal Hawaiian Hotel, was built by the Matson Navigation Company to accommodate travelers arriving on luxury liners. It was opened with a grand ball, and Waikīkī was officially launched as a first-class tourist destination—duck ponds, taro patches, and all.

December 7, 1941, brought that era to a close, with the bombing of Pearl Harbor and America's entry into the war in the Pacific. The Royal Hawaiian was turned over to American military forces and became a respite for war-weary soldiers and sailors. But with victory came the postwar boom, and by 1952 Waikīkī had 2,000 hotel rooms. Today, hundreds of thousands of visitors sleep in the more than 33,000 rooms of Waikīkī's nearly 160 hotels and condominiums. Waikīkī continues to serve as home base for endless possibilities for day trips full of cultural and scenic eco-adventures. Visitors can stroll along a new and improved Kūhiō Beach and find wider beach expanses and extensive services, and meander along the historic Waikīkī walking trail. There are free nightly Hawaiian music and dance performances on the Kūhiō Beach stage. A massive redesign of the Kalia Road and Beachwalk area is scheduled to start in late 2002 and be completed in 2006. Here, Outrigger Enterprises plans to turn its older hotels from the 1960s into one modern hotel, retail, and entertainment complex. With Waikīkī leading the way, O'ahu maintains its status as an exciting destination, with more things to see, more places to eat, and more things to do than on all the other Hawaiian Islands combined.

PLEASURES AND PASTIMES

BEACHES

To many O'ahu's Waikīkī Beach epitomizes Hawai'i's beach culture. This hotel-studded strip is tough to beat for convenience to restaurants and shopping, but the big waves are on the North Shore's Sunset Beach and along Waimea Bay. Kailua Beach Park is the site of international windsurfing competitions; its neighbor, Lanikai Beach is often referred to as the most beautiful beach in the world; and, Makapu'u Beach, near Sea Life Park, has some of the best bodysurfing in the state.

DINING

O'ahu's cuisines are as diverse as its population, with Asian, European, and Pacific flavors most prevalent. Here, the Asian influence can even be found at the corner fast-food restaurant, where the McDonald's menu is posted in both English and kanji. While you're exploring O'ahu's banquet of choices, be sure to sample Hawai'i regional cuisine, also known variously as Euro-Asian or Pacific Rim.

LODGING

O'ahu's lodgings range from sprawling resorts that seem to be cities unto themselves to intimate, low-rise hideaways. First-time visitors who wish to be in the heart of the island's activity can find it all in Waikīkī. Guests do well by this south shore tourist mecca, since shops, restaurants, nightlife, and the beach are all just a stroll away. Business travelers prefer to stay on the eastern edge of Waikīkī, near the Hawai'i Convention Center, or in Downtown Honolulu's sole hotel. Windward and North Shore digs are casual and shorter on amenities but have charms all their own.

Your checklist for a perfect journey

WAY AHEAD
- Devise a trip budget.

- Write down the five things you want most from this trip. Keep this list handy before and during your trip.

- Make plane or train reservations. Book lodging and rental cars.

- Arrange for pet care.

- Check your passport. Apply for a new one if necessary.

- Photocopy important documents and store in a safe place.

A MONTH BEFORE
- Make restaurant reservations and buy theater and concert tickets. Visit fodors.com for links to local events.

- Familiarize yourself with the local language or lingo.

TWO WEEKS BEFORE
- Replenish your supply of medications.

- Create your itinerary.

- Enjoy a book or movie set in your destination to get you in the mood.

- Develop a packing list. Shop for missing essentials. Repair and launder or dry-clean your clothes.

A WEEK BEFORE
- Stop newspaper deliveries. Pay bills.

- Acquire traveler's checks.

- Stock up on film.

- Label your luggage.

- Finalize your packing list— take less than you think you need.

- Create a toiletries kit filled with travel-size essentials.

- Get lots of sleep. Don't get sick before your trip.

A DAY BEFORE
- Drink plenty of water.

- Check your travel documents.

- Get packing!

DURING YOUR TRIP
- Keep a journal/scrapbook.

- Spend time with locals.

- Take time to explore. Don't plan too much.

LŪʻAU

Just about everyone who comes to Hawaiʻi goes to at least one lūʻau. Traditionally, lūʻau last for days, with feasts, sporting events, hula, and song. But at today's scaled-down version you're as likely to find macaroni salad on the buffet as poi, and heaps of fried chicken beside kālua pig.

If you want authenticity, look in the newspaper to see if a church or civic club is holding a lūʻau fund-raiser. You'll not only be welcome, you'll experience some downhome Hawaiiana.

SURFING

Surfers from around the world come to ride Hawaiʻi's formidable waves, including the bone-rattling Banzai Pipeline. Indeed, Oʻahu's North Shore is an excellent place to view the veterans, especially during high-surf in December and January. For first-time surfers, Waikīkī Beach is probably the best spot to pick up the basics; there are plenty of schools staffed by experienced local surfers who will be happy to show you the ropes.

In This Chapter

Updated by Maggie Wunsch

here and there

IF HAWAI'I IS AMERICA'S MOST EXOTIC, most unique state, then Waikīkī is its generator, keeping everything humming. On the dry, sunny side of O'ahu, it incorporates all the natural splendors of the Islands and synthesizes them with elegance and daring into an international playground in the middle of the Pacific.

Throughout Downtown Honolulu, past and present play a delightful counterpoint. Modern skyscrapers stand directly across from the Aloha Tower, which was built in 1926 and was, until the early 1960s, the tallest structure in Honolulu. Old structures have found new meaning here. For instance, today's governor's mansion, built in 1846, was the home of Queen Lili'uokalani until her death in 1917.

It all lies in the shadow of Diamond Head crater, perhaps Hawai'i's most famous natural landmark. Diamond Head got its name from sailors who thought they had found precious gems on its slopes. The diamonds proved to be volcanic refuse.

WAIKĪKĪ

Waikīkī sparkles along 2½ mi of spangled sea from the famous Diamond Head crater on the east to the Ala Wai Yacht Harbor on the west. Separated on its northern boundary from the sprawling city of Honolulu by the broad Ala Wai Canal, Waikīkī is 3½ mi from Downtown Honolulu and worlds apart from any other city in the world. You may find yourself saying such things as *aloha* and *mahalo* (thank you), and don't be surprised if you find yourself

honolulu including waikīkī

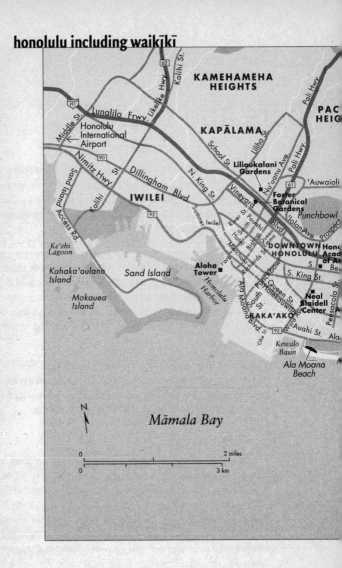

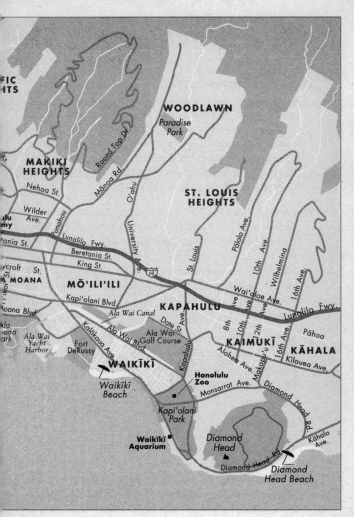

planning your next trip back as you laze on its sunny, hypnotic shores.

Sights to See

① ALA WAI YACHT HARBOR. Every other summer the Trans-Pacific yacht race from Los Angeles makes its colorful finish here, complete with flags and onboard parties. The next Trans-Pac is estimated to arrive in July of 2003. No matter when you visit Hawai'i, if you want a taste of what life on the water could be like, stroll around the docks and check out the variety of craft, from houseboats to luxury cruisers. *1777 Ala Moana Blvd., oceanside across from Renaissance 'Ilikai Waikīkī, Waikīkī.*

⑬ DAMIEN MUSEUM. This tiny two-room museum behind St. Augustine's Church contains low-key exhibits about Father Damien, the Belgian priest who worked with those afflicted with Hansen's disease (leprosy) who were exiled to the Hawaiian island of Moloka'i during the late 1800s. Ask to see the museum's 20-minute videotape. It's low-budget but well done and emotionally gripping. *130 'Ōhua Ave., Waikīkī, tel. 808/923–2690. Free. Weekdays 9–3.*

⑤ FIRST HAWAIIAN BANK. Get a glimpse of Hawaiian history kept safe in this Waikīkī bank, where half a dozen murals depict the evolution of Hawaiian culture. The impressive panels were painted between 1951 and 1952 by Jean Charlot (1898–1979), whose work is represented in Florence at the Uffizi Gallery and in New York at both the Metropolitan Museum and the Museum of Modern Art. The murals are beautifully lit at night, with some panels visible from the street. *2181 Kalākaua Ave., Waikīkī, tel. 808/943–4670. Free. Mon.–Thurs. 8:30–4, Fri. 8:30–6.*

⑥ GUMP BUILDING. Built in 1929 in Hawaiian-colonial style, with Asian architectural motifs and a blue-tile roof, this structure once housed Hawai'i's premier store, Gump's, which was known for high-quality Asian and Hawaiian objects. It's now home to a Louis Vuitton boutique. 2200 Kalākaua Ave., Waikīkī.

⑦ HALEKŪLANI. Maintaining an air of mystery within its tranquil setting, the modern Halekūlani is centered around a portion of its original (1917) beachfront estate, immortalized as the setting for the first of the Charlie Chan detective novels, *The House Without a Key*. For a view of an orchid blossom unlike any other, take a peek at the swimming pool with its huge orchid mosaic on the bottom. 2199 Kālia Rd., Waikīkī, tel. 808/923–2311.

② HILTON HAWAIIAN VILLAGE BEACH RESORT AND SPA. With a little island in Kahanamoku Lagoon and palm trees all around, this 20-acre Waikīkī resort is the quintessential tropical getaway. The village is a hodgepodge of Asian architecture, with a Chinese moon gate, a pagoda, and a Japanese farmhouse with a waterwheel, all dominated by a tall mosaic mural of the hotel's Rainbow Tower. You can browse for souvenirs in all price ranges at the **Rainbow Bazaar,** which has 90 different specialty stores. The Kalia Tower is home to a miniature version of Bishop Museum and designed to give visitors an interactive glimpse of the history of Polynesia. 2005 Kālia Rd., Waikīkī, tel. 808/949–4321.

⑨ IMAX WAIKĪKĪ THEATER. Immerse yourself in a view of "Hidden Hawai'i" among other film features on a screen five stories high and 70 ft wide; digital surround sound completes the experience. Call or consult local newspapers for shows and times. 325 Seaside Ave., Waikīkī, tel. 808/923–4629, www.imaxwaikiki.com. $9.75, $13.75 for double feature. Daily, call for show times.

⑩ INTERNATIONAL MARKET PLACE. The tropical open-air setting is fun to wander through, with wood-carvers, basket-weavers, and other artisans from various Pacific islands hawking their handicrafts. Intrepid shoppers find fun souvenirs here, and at the adjacent Duke's Lane. Free hula performances are given on Monday and Wednesday–Saturday. 2330 Kalākaua Ave., Waikīkī, tel. 808/923–9871.

waikīkī

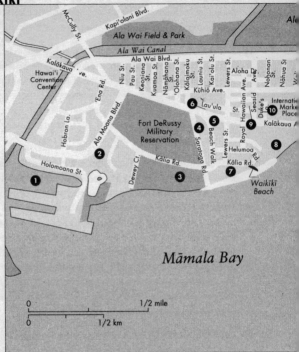

Māmala Bay

0 — 1/2 mile
0 — 1/2 km

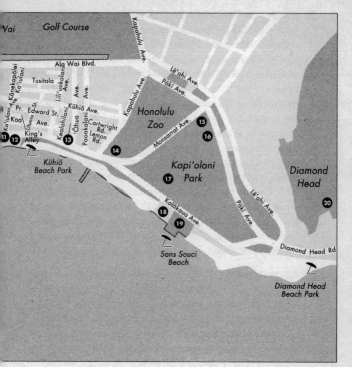

⑫ KAHUNA (WIZARD) STONES OF WAIKĪKĪ. According to legend, these boulders preserve the magnetic legacy of four Tahitian sorcerers—Kapaemahu, Kinohi, Kapuni, and Kahaloa. Just to the west of these revered rocks is the **Duke Kahanamoku Statue,** erected in honor of Hawai'i's celebrated surfer and swimmer. Known as the "father of modern surfing," Duke won his first gold medal for the 100-m freestyle at the 1912 Olympics. When the bronze statue was first placed here, it caused a wave of controversy, as the Duke is facing away from the water with his back to the ocean, something no safety-conscious surfer would ever do. Check out the standing bronze surfboard next to the statue; it's one of several markers that can be found throughout Waikīkī as part of the historic Waikīkī walking trail. Free 90-minute guided walking tours begin at the statue at 9 AM weekdays and 4:30 PM Saturday. *Waikīkī Beach, Diamond Head side of Sheraton Moana Surfrider, Waikīkī, tel. 808/841–6442, www. waikikihistorictrail.com.*

⑧ ROYAL HAWAIIAN HOTEL. This legendary hotel sticks out amid the high-rises on Waikīkī Beach like a pink confection. Affectionately nicknamed the Pink Palace, the Royal Hawaiian opened in 1927, and the lobby is reminiscent of an era when visitors to the Islands arrived on luxury liners. A stroll through the Royal's coconut grove garden is like a walk back to a time when Waikīkī was still a sleepy, tropical paradise. *2259 Kalākaua Ave., Waikīkī, tel. 808/923–7311.*

★ ⑪ SHERATON MOANA SURFRIDER. Listed on the National Register of Historic Places, this intricate beaux arts–style hotel was christened "The First Lady of Waikīkī" when she opened her doors at the turn of the 20th century. With period furnishings and historical exhibits, this landmark holds plenty of Hawai'i nostalgia. Visit the **Historical Room** in the rotunda above the main entrance to see the collection of old photographs and memorabilia dating from the opening of the hotel. Then take afternoon high tea on the **Banyan Veranda.** *2365 Kalākaua Ave., Waikīkī, tel. 808/922–3111.*

4 **THE URASENKE FOUNDATION.** The tea house here was the first of its kind to be built outside Japan (it was built in 1951). If you are looking for a slice of serenity in Waikīkī, this is a good place to find it. The meditative ceremony reflects the influences of centuries of Zen Buddhism. Each ceremony lasts approximately 30 minutes; you can participate or just watch. Wear something comfortable enough for sitting on the floor (but no shorts, please). *245 Saratoga Rd., Waikīkī, tel. 808/923–3059. Minimum donation $3. Wed. and Fri. 10–noon.*

 3 **U.S. ARMY MUSEUM.** This museum at Ft. DeRussy houses an intimidating collection of war memorabilia. The major focus is on World War II, but exhibits range from ancient Hawaiian weaponry to displays relating to the Vietnam War. It's within Battery Randolf (Building 32), a bunker built in 1911 as a key to the defense of Pearl Harbor and Honolulu. Some of its walls are 22 ft thick. Guided group tours can be arranged. *Ft. DeRussy, Bldg. 32, Kālia Rd., Waikīkī, tel. 808/438–2822. Free. Tues.–Sun. 10–4:30.*

KAPI'OLANI PARK AND DIAMOND HEAD

Kapi'olani Park, established during the late 1800s by King Kalākaua and named after his queen, is a 500-acre expanse where you can play all sorts of sports, enjoy a picnic, see wild animals, or hear live music. Working your way up to the Diamond Head's summit, whether on foot or by car, is well worth the effort, though there are plenty of pleasant strolls around the base.

Sights to See

★ **20** **DIAMOND HEAD.** Panoramas from this 760-ft extinct volcanic peak, once used as a military fortification, sweep from across Waikīkī and Honolulu in one direction and out to Koko Head in the other, with surfers and windsurfers scattered like confetti on the cresting waves below. This ideal 360-degree O'ahu perspective is great for first-time visitors. Most guidebooks say there are 99 steps on the trail to the top. That's true of one flight, but there are four flights altogether. Bring a flashlight to see your way through a narrow tunnel and up a very dark flight of winding stairs. And take bottled water with you to ensure that you stay hydrated under the tropical sun. *Monsarrat Ave. at 18th Ave., Waikīkī. $1. Daily 6–6.*

⑭ HONOLULU ZOO. There are bigger and better zoos, but this one is pretty, and on Wednesday evening in summer, the zoo puts on "The Wildest Show in Town," a free concert series. The best part of the zoo is its 7½-acre African savanna, where animals roam freely on the other side of hidden rails and moats. If you're visiting during a full moon, check out the "Zoo by Moonlight" tours to get a glimpse of animals who are active only by starlight. *151 Kapahulu Ave., Waikīkī, tel. 808/971–7171, www.honoluluzoo.org. $6. Daily 9–4:30.*

⑰ KAPIʻOLANI BANDSTAND. A replica of the Victorian Kapiʻolani Bandstand, which was originally built in the late 1890s, is Kapiʻolani Park's centerpiece for community entertainment and concerts. Check out the "Bandstand Jams," held at 5:30 every Friday, with concert performances ranging from contemporary Hawaiian to jazz to reggae. Local newspapers list entertainment information. *ʻEwa end of Kapiʻolani Park, mauka side of Kalākaua Ave., Waikīkī.*

★ ⑯ PLEASANT HAWAIIAN HULA SHOW. This one-hour show, in the bleachers adjacent to the Waikīkī Shell, is colorful, lively, and fun. It has been wowing crowds since 1937. For the best viewpoints, come early for good seating. *2805 Monsarrat Ave., Waikīkī, tel. 808/945–1851. Free. Tues.–Thurs. at 10.*

★ ⑱ WAIKĪKĪ AQUARIUM. This amazing little attraction harbors more than 300 species of Hawaiian and South Pacific marine life, the only chambered nautilus living in captivity, and sharks. The Edge of the Reef exhibit showcases five different types of reef environments found along Hawaiʻi's shorelines. Check out the Sea Visions Theater, the biodiversity exhibit, and the audio tour.

2777 Kalākaua Ave., Waikīkī, tel. 808/923–9741, www.waquarium.org.
$7. Daily 9–5.

⑮ WAIKĪKĪ SHELL. Local people bring a picnic and get "grass seats"
(lawn seating). Here's a chance to enjoy a magical night
underneath the stars with some of Hawai'i's best musicians as
well as visiting guest artists. Concerts are held May 1 to Labor Day.
Check the newspapers to see what's playing. 2805 Monsarrat
Ave., Waikīkī, tel. 808/924–8934.

⑲ WAIKĪKĪ WAR MEMORIAL NATATORIUM. This 1927 World War
I monument stands proudly, its outer wall lighted at night,
showing off a newly restored entrance facade. The 100-m saltwater
swimming pool is closed to the public. 2777 Kalākaua Ave., Waikīkī.

DOWNTOWN HONOLULU

To reach Downtown Honolulu from Waikīkī by car, take Ala
Moana Boulevard to Alakea Street. There are public parking lots
(50¢ per half hour for the first two hours) in buildings along
Alakea Street and Bethel Street, two blocks 'ewa. Keep in mind
that parking in most downtown lots is expensive ($3 per half
hour).

Sights to See

㉒ ALOHA TOWER MARKETPLACE. Two stories of shops, kiosks,
indoor and outdoor restaurants, and live entertainment are here
at the Honolulu Harbor with Aloha Tower as its anchor. For a bird's-
eye view of this working harbor, take the free ride up to the
tower's observation deck. The Marketplace's location makes it
an ideal spot for watching the arrival of cruise ships. On Hawaiian
Boat Days, the waterfront comes alive with entertainment and
hula dancers who greet the arriving ships. 1 Aloha Tower Dr., at Piers
8, 9, and 10, Downtown Honolulu, tel. 808/528–5700. Daily 9–9,
restaurants 9 AM–2 AM.

downtown honolulu

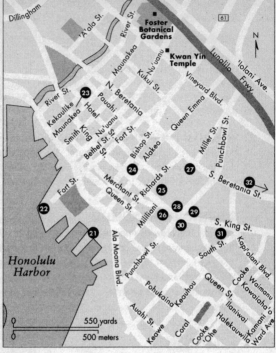

㉓ CHINATOWN. Noodle factories and herb shops, lei stands and acupuncture studios, art galleries and Chinese and Thai restaurants make up this historic neighborhood, which has experienced a recent surge in restoration. A major highlight is the colorful O'ahu Market, an open-air emporium with hanging pigs' heads, display cases of fresh fish, row after row of exotic fruits and vegetables, and vendors of all ethnic backgrounds. Check out the Chinese Cultural Plaza's Moongate stage for cultural events, especially around the Chinese New Year. *King St. between Smith and River Sts., Chinatown.*

 ㉑ HAWAI'I MARITIME CENTER. The main exhibits, some of which are interactive, at this maritime museum are in the **Kalākaua Boat House,** where you can learn about Hawai'i's whaling days, the history of Honolulu Harbor, the Clipper seaplane, and surfing and windsurfing in Hawai'i. Moored next to the Boat House are the *Falls of Clyde,* a century-old, four-masted, square-rigged ship that once brought tea from China to the U.S. west coast, now used as a museum; and the *Hōkūle'a,* a reproduction of an ancient Polynesian double-hull voyaging canoe. The *Hōkūle'a* has completed several journeys throughout the Pacific, during which the crew used only the stars and the sea as navigational guides. *Ala Moana Blvd., at Pier 7, Downtown Honolulu, tel. 808/536–6373. $7.50. Daily 8:30–8.*

㉗ HAWAI'I STATE CAPITOL. The capitol's architecture is richly symbolic: the columns look like palm trees, the legislative chambers are shaped like volcanic cinder cones, and the central court is open to the sky, representing Hawai'i's open society. The building is surrounded by reflecting pools, just as the Islands are embraced by water. *215 S. Beretania St., Downtown Honolulu, tel. 808/586–0146. Free. Guided tours upon request weekday afternoons.*

㉘ HAWAI'I STATE LIBRARY. This beautifully renovated main library, originally built in 1913, is wonderful to explore. Its "Asia and the Pacific" room has a fascinating collection of books old and new about Hawai'i. The center courtyard offers a respite from busy downtown. *478 King St., Downtown Honolulu, tel. 808/586–3500. Free. Mon. and Fri.–Sat. 9–5, Tues. and Thurs. 9–8, Wed. 10–5.*

32 HONOLULU ACADEMY OF ARTS. The academy dates to 1927 and has an impressive permanent collection that includes Hiroshige's ukiyo-e Japanese prints, donated by James Michener; Italian Renaissance paintings; and American and European art. Six open-air courtyards provide a casual counterpart to the more formal interior galleries. The Luce Pavilion complex houses a traveling-exhibit gallery, a Hawaiian gallery, a café, and a gift shop. The Academy Theatre offers a variety of art films. If interested in Islamic art, inquire about the select tour offerings from the academy's art center to the Doris Duke Foundation for Islamic Art, located within Duke's former Diamond Head estate. At this writing, the late heiress's mansion was scheduled to open to the public in late 2002. Call about special exhibits, concerts, and films. *900 S. Beretania St., Downtown Honolulu, tel. 808/532–8700, www. honoluluacademy.org. $7. Tues.–Sat. 10–4:30, Sun. 1–5.*

29 HONOLULU HALE. This Mediterranean Renaissance–style building was constructed in 1929 and serves as the center of city government. Stroll through the cool, open-ceiling lobby with exhibits of local artists, and time your visit to coincide with one of the free concerts sometimes offered in the evening, when the building stays open late. During the winter holiday season, the Hale becomes the focal point for the annual Honolulu City Lights Festival program. *530 S. King St., Downtown Honolulu, Free. Weekdays 8–4:30.*

25 'IOLANI PALACE. Built in 1882 on the site of an earlier palace and beautifully restored, this is America's only royal residence. It contains the thrones of King Kalākaua and his successor (and sister) Queen Lili'uokalani. Downstairs galleries showcase the royal jewelry, kitchen, and offices of the monarchy. The palace is open for guided tours only, and reservations are essential. Take a look at the gift shop, formerly the 'Iolani Barracks, built to house the Royal Guard. *King and Richards Sts., Downtown Honolulu, tel. 808/ 522–0832. $15. Tues.–Sat. 9–2:15.*

26 **KAMEHAMEHA I STATUE.** This downtown landmark pays tribute to the Big Island chieftain who united all the warring Hawaiian Islands into one kingdom at the turn of the 18th century. He stands with one arm outstretched in welcome. The original version is in Kapa'au, on the Big Island, near the king's birthplace. Each year on June 11, his birthday, the statue is draped in lei. *417 S. King St., outside Ali'iōlani Hale, Downtown Honolulu.*

30 **KAWAIAHA'O CHURCH.** Fancifully called Hawai'i's Westminster Abbey, this 14,000-coral-block house of worship witnessed the coronations, weddings, and funerals of generations of Hawaiian royalty. The graves of missionaries and of King Lunalilo are in the yard. The upper gallery has an exhibit of paintings of the royal families. Services in English and Hawaiian are held each Sunday. Although there are no guided tours, you can look around the church at no cost. *957 Punchbowl St., at King St., Downtown Honolulu, tel. 808/522–1333. Free. Service Sun. at 8 AM, in Hawaiian at 10:30 AM, Wed. at 6 PM.*

31 **MISSION HOUSES MUSEUM.** The stalwart Hawai'i missionaries arrived in 1820, gaining royal favor and influencing every aspect of island life. Their descendants became leaders in government and business. You can walk through their original dwellings, including a white-frame house that was prefabricated in New England, shipped around the Horn, and is Hawai'i's oldest wooden structure. The museum hosts living history programs, candlelight museum tours, and crafts fairs. Certain areas of the museum may be seen only on a one-hour guided tour. *553 S. King St., Downtown Honolulu, tel. 808/531–0481, www.lava.net/~mhm. $8. Tues.–Sat. 9–4; guided tours at 9:45, 11:15, 1, and 2:30.*

24 **TAMARIND PARK.** From jazz and Hawaiian tunes to the strains of the U.S. Marine Band, music fills this pretty park at noon on Friday. Do as the locals do: pick up lunch at one of the many carryout restaurants and find a bench or patch of grass. *S. King St. between Bishop and Alakea Sts., Downtown Honolulu. Free.*

In This Chapter

Updated by Maggie Wunsch

eating out

IF YOU'RE LOOKING FOR A MEAL WITH A VIEW, explore the restaurants at the upscale hotels and resorts that line O'ahu's shores. Settings can be as casual as a "barefoot bar" or as elegant as a romantic dinner for two under the stars. Beyond Waikīkī are culinary jewels tucked away in shopping centers and residential neighborhoods that specialize in ethnic cuisines. You'll almost never go wrong if you sample the offerings at any establishment whose name ends in the words "Drive Inn." Here you will find the local grinds, which are the staples of the Hawaiian diet: seafood plate lunches and noodle saimin soups. For snacks and fast food around the island, look for the lunch wagons, usually parked roadside near the beaches.

SPECIALTIES

Fish, fruit, and fresh island-grown produce are the base of Hawai'i regional cuisine. The "plate lunch" is the heart of most Hawaiians' days and usually consists of grilled teriyaki chicken, beef, or fish, served with two scoops of white rice and two side salads. Poke, marinated raw tuna, is a local hallmark.

CATEGORY	COST*
$$$$	over $45
$$$	$30–$45
$$	$15–$30
$	$5–$15

*per person for a main course at dinner

WAIKĪKĪ

Chinese

$$ GOLDEN DRAGON. Nearly 65 à la carte dishes and a six-course
★ dinner make up the menu of fine Cantonese, Szechuan, and
nouvelle-Chinese dishes prepared by chef Steve Chiang. Signature
dishes include stir-fried lobster with curry sauce and Szechuan
beef. Two of the house specialties—the Imperial Peking duck
and Imperial beggar's chicken (whole chicken wrapped in lotus
leaves and baked in a clay pot)—must be ordered 24 hours in
advance. *Hilton Hawaiian Village, 2005 Kālia Rd., Waikīkī, tel. 808/
946–5336. Reservations essential. AE, D, DC, MC, V. No lunch.*

Contemporary

$$–$$$ BALI BY THE SEA. In the Hilton Hawaiian Village, this restaurant
★ is breeze-swept, with an oceanside setting offering glorious views
of Waikīkī Beach. Chef Jean-Luc Voegele's menu is a blend of French
and Asian influences, with such entrées as casserole of Hawaiian
lobster and ʻōpakapaka (blue snapper) with Kaffir lime sauce.
Another favorite is the roasted-beet salad with carmelized
macadamia nuts and goat cheese. *Hilton Hawaiian Village, 2005
Kālia Rd., Waikīkī, tel. 808/941–2254. Reservations essential. AE, D, DC,
MC, V. No dinner Sun.*

$$–$$$ DIAMOND HEAD GRILL. A mix of Asian, Euro-American, and
Polynesian influences come together to mark the cuisine at this
grill, which is in the sleek W Honolulu–Diamond Head. For
breakfast, try the macadamia-and-ginger waffles with *pohā*-berry
butter (pohā is Hawaiian for cape gooseberry). Dinner entrées
include hearty beefs, and guava-and-mustard-crusted rack of
lamb. The hip DHG Bar serves up "mai tai martinis" and features
a plush W-style bed as accent seating. *W Honolulu–Diamond Head
Hotel, 2885 Kalākaua Ave., Waikīkī, tel. 808/922–3734. Reservations
essential. AE, D, MC, V. No lunch.*

$$–$$$ HAU TREE LĀNAI. At breakfast, lunch, or dinner you can eat under graceful hau trees, so close to Kaimana Beach you can hear the whisper of the waves. Breakfast offerings include a huge helping of eggs Benedict, poi pancakes, or a delicious salmon omelet. For dinner, try the moonfish, snapper, the seafood mixed grill in Thai chili sauce, or the popular sesame-crusted hoisin rack of lamb. *New Otani Kaimana Beach Hotel, 2863 Kalākaua Ave., Waikīkī, tel. 808/921–7066. Reservations essential. AE, D, DC, MC, V.*

$–$$ DUKE'S CANOE CLUB. Beachfront in the Outrigger Waikīkī, and named after Hawai'i's famous surfer Duke Kahanamoku, this eatery is casual and usually crowded (reserve ahead or you'll probably have to wait for a table). Weekend evenings the restaurant hosts sunset "concerts on the beach" on its outdoor terrace. Seafood and steak are at the heart of the menu, and prices are moderate. Fish can be served up Duke's style, which is baked in a garlic, lemon, and sweet basil glaze to keep it tender and moist. Other Duke's specialties include Caesar salad, macadamia-and-crab wontons, and the decadent Hula Pie. *Outrigger Waikīkī on the Beach, 2335 Kalākaua Ave., Waikīkī, tel. 808/922–2268. AE, D, DC, MC, V.*

$–$$ HOUSE WITHOUT A KEY. This is one of the jewels of Waikīkī, a casual seaside spot in the serene Halekūlani hotel serving salads, sandwiches, and hearty meals. Favorites include Joy's Sandwich (crabmeat salad, bacon, and avocado on whole wheat bread) and the beef burger on a kaiser roll. With the ocean and Diamond Head in view, this is a mesmerizing place at sunset, when hula dancing and Hawaiian music say "aloha" to the day's end. A breakfast buffet is served daily between 7 and 10:30. *Halekūlani, 2199 Kālia Rd., Waikīkī, tel. 808/923–2311. Reservations not accepted. AE, MC, V.*

French

$$$ LA MER. In the exotic, oceanfront atmosphere of a Mandalay
★ mansion, you'll be served neoclassic French cuisine that many

waikīkī dining

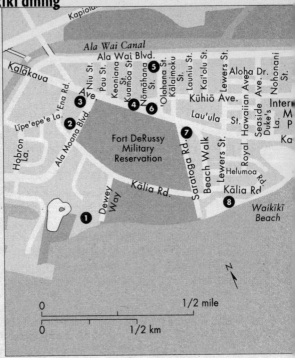

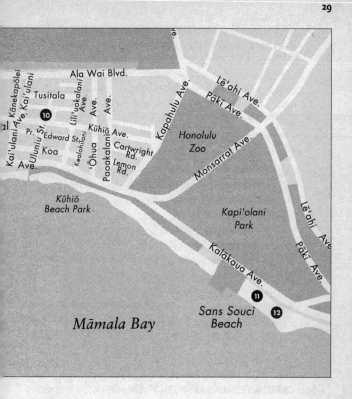

consider to be the finest in Hawai'i. Here, on the grounds of the Halekūlani, is a room—open to the ocean, and with sweeping views of Diamond Head—as luscious as its menu. Begin your meal with tartares of *hamachi* (yellowtail), 'ahi (yellowfin tuna), and salmon with three caviars. For your entrée, dive into the lobster mosaic with fresh hearts of palm and osetra caviar. A favorite sweet is the symphony of four desserts. *Halekūlani, 2199 Kālia Rd., Waikīkī, tel. 808/923–2311. Reservations essential. Jacket required. AE, MC, V. No lunch.*

\$\$-\$\$\$ ★ PADOVANI'S RESTAURANT AND WINE BAR. Philippe Padovani gained fame at three top Hawai'i hotels (Halekūlani, Ritz-Carlton, and Mānele Bay) before opening his own place in the Doubletree Alana Waikīkī. One of the chef's specialties is the salmon confit in extra-virgin olive oil and lemongrass broth. Seafood lovers will also savor the sautéed tiger shrimp served with mushroom-herb polenta and tomato and basil sauce. An upstairs wine bar offers 50 varietals by the glass, single-malt Scotches, a lighter menu, entertainment on weekend evenings, and an enclosed cigar room. A prix fixe menu is \$45. *Doubletree Alana Waikīkī, 1956 Ala Moana Blvd., Waikīkī, tel. 808/946–3456 or 808/947–1236. Reservations essential. AE, D, DC, MC, V.*

Italian

\$\$\$ CAFFELATTE ITALIAN RESTAURANT. Every dish at this tiny trattoria is worth ordering, from the gnocchi in a thick, rich sauce of Gorgonzola cheese to the veal scallopini in a light white wine sauce sprinkled with parsley. The tiramisu is the best in town. A family from Milan operates this restaurant with limited seating inside and a few tables outside on the narrow lānai. Be aware that each person must order three courses (appetizer, main course, and dessert). The chef will prepare a special mystery dinner for two for \$60. There's no parking, so walk here if you can. *339 Saratoga Rd., 2nd level, Waikīkī, tel. 808/924–1414. AE, DC, MC, V. Closed Tues.*

Japanese

$$-$$$ **SHIZU.** Sample the Japanese cooking styles of *teishoku* (traditional Japanese preparation of fish, rice, soup, and more, served in lacquer bowls) and tableside *teppanyaki* in a contemporary setting overlooking a Zen-style rock garden. The two teppanyaki rooms have spectacular stained-glass windows with vibrant irises. Here, diners sit around a massive iron grill on which a dexterous chef slices and cooks sizzling meats and vegetables. There's also a sushi bar and traditional dishes such as tempura. Try green-tea cheesecake for dessert. *Royal Garden at Waikīkī, 440 'Olohana St., 4th floor, Waikīkī, tel. 808/943–0202. AE, D, DC, MC, V.*

Seafood

$$-$$$$ **NICK'S FISHMARKET.** The decor is a little dark and retro, with black
★ booths, candlelight, and formal table settings. But here you can indulge in Beluga caviar, oysters Rockefeller, and a sumptuous sourdough lobster bisque. In addition, this is one of the few places with abalone on the menu; it's sautéed and served with lobster risotto. Leave room for Vanbana Pie, a decadent combination of bananas, vanilla Swiss-almond ice cream, and hot caramel sauce. *Waikīkī Gateway Hotel, 2070 Kalākaua Ave., Waikīkī, tel. 808/955–6333. Reservations essential. AE, D, DC, MC, V.*

$$-$$$ **ORCHIDS.** It seems only fitting that you can hear the waves from
★ this orchid-filled dining room that lays out the best seafood bar in town, including sashimi, *poke* (marinated raw fish), and shellfish. Try the pistachio-crusted *hapuupūu* (sea bass) and the seafood curries. Meat and poultry dishes include a mustard-herb roasted Colorado lamb rack and tandoori-roasted island chicken. Outdoor and indoor seating is available, with the best views from the lānai. *Halekūlani, 2199 Kālia Rd., Waikīkī, tel. 808/923–2311. Reservations essential. AE, MC, V.*

$-$$ **TODAI.** Long on seafood and short on decor, this restaurant is still
★ a hit with both local residents and tourists alike. Todai has a

180-ft seafood buffet with 40 different kinds of sushi that include salmon skin, sea urchin, eel, and spicy tuna. You'll also find lobster, shrimp tempura, Alaskan snow crab, salad, barbecued ribs, and much more on the buffet. Save room for a "Tokyo" crepe filled with fresh fruit and chocolate filling, topped with whipped cream. 1910 Ala Moana Blvd., Waikīkī, tel. 808/947–1000. *Reservations essential. AE, D, DC, MC, V.*

Steak

$$–$$$$ **HY'S STEAK HOUSE.** Things always seem to go well at Hy's, from the filet mignon tartare and oysters Rockefeller right through to the flaming desserts. The atmosphere is snug and librarylike, and you can watch the chef perform behind glass. Hy's is famous for its kiawe-broiled New York strip steak, beef Wellington, cold-water lobster tail, and rack of lamb. The Caesar salad is excellent, as are the panfried O'Brien potatoes. *Waikīkī Park Heights Hotel, 2440 Kūhiō Ave., Waikīkī, tel. 808/922–5555. Reservations essential. AE, DC, MC, V. No lunch.*

Thai

$–$$ **SINGHA THAI CUISINE.** Dishes here are prepared in traditional
★ Thai fashion, with just a sprinkling of Hawaiian regional flavorings. The blackened tuna summer rolls, vegetarian curry dishes, and Thai chili are wonderful. Singha's beautiful Royal Thai dancers dressed in traditional costume add to the occasion, performing nightly center stage in the restaurant. *1910 Ala Moana Blvd., Waikīkī, tel. 808/941–2898. Reservations essential. AE, D, DC, MC, V. No lunch.*

$ **KEO'S IN WAIKĪKĪ.** This little twinkling nook, with tables set
★ amid lighted trees, big paper umbrellas, and sprays of orchids, is a favorite of visiting Hollywood celebrities. Most of the herbs, vegetables, fruits, and flowers found here are grown on owner Keo Sananikone's North Shore farm. Favorites include the Evil Jungle Prince (shrimp, vegetables, or chicken in a sauce flavored with

basil, coconut milk, and red chili). Consider ordering your food mild or medium: it'll still be hot. For dessert, the apple bananas (small, tart bananas grown in Hawai'i) in coconut milk are wonderful. *2028 Kūhiō Ave., Waikīkī, tel. 808/951–9355. Reservations essential. AE, D, DC, MC, V. No lunch.*

HONOLULU

American/Casual

$–$$ CALIFORNIA PIZZA KITCHEN. This duet of dining and watering holes for young fast-trackers is worth the likely wait for a table. The pizzas have unusual toppings, such as Thai chicken, Peking duck, and Caribbean shrimp. The pastas are made fresh daily. At the Kāhala site, a glass atrium with tiled and mirrored walls and one side open to the shopping mall creates a sidewalk-café effect. The location on the top level of the Ala Moana Center offers a great respite for the weary shopper. *Kāhala Mall, 4211 Wai'alae Ave., Kāhala, tel. 808/737–9446; Ala Moana Shopping Center, 1450 Ala Moana Blvd., Ala Moana, tel. 808/941–7715. Reservations not accepted. AE, D, DC, MC, V.*

$–$$ HARD ROCK CAFE. The Honolulu branch of this international chain has its trademark rock-and-roll memorabilia on display along with Hawaiian surfboards and aloha shirts for added local flavor. Hard Rock has always sold more T-shirts than T-bones, so don't expect culinary surprises. Here charbroiled burgers, tupelo chicken, and barbecue ribs are old standards, but don't overlook the 'ahi steak sandwiches or the watermelon baby-back ribs. Count on the sound system being loud, the energy being high, and the wait for a table during peak hours being long. *1837 Kapi'olani Blvd., Ala Moana, tel. 808/955–7383. Reservations not accepted. AE, MC, V.*

$ L & L DRIVE INN. In the Kāhala Mall, and at more than 50 neighborhood locations throughout the island, the "drive inn" serves up an impressive mix of Asian-American and Hawaiian-style plate lunches. Chicken *katsu* (cutlet), beef curry, and seafood

honolulu dining

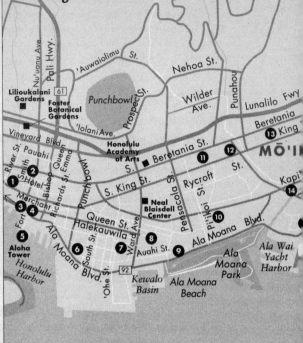

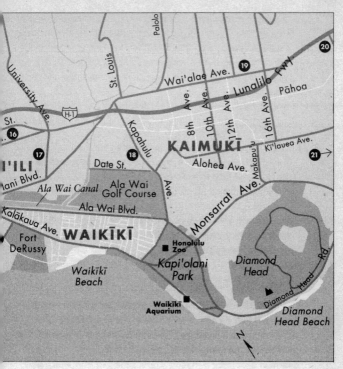

mix plates include two scoops of rice and macaroni salad. There are also "mini" versions of the large-portion plates that include just one scoop of starch. It's a quick take-out place to pick up lunch before heading to the nearest beach park. *Kāhala Mall, 4211 Waialae Ave., Kāhala, tel. 808/732–4042. Reservations not accepted. No credit cards.*

Barbecue

$–$$ DIXIE GRILL. This Southern-inspired eatery emphasizes just how much fun food can be. Why, there's even an outdoor sandbox for the kids! Dixie Grill specializes in all-things-fried, including okra, catfish, and chicken. Also on the menu are baby-back ribs, whole Dungeness crab, and campfire steak. Recipes for the barbecue sauces come from Memphis, the Carolinas, Georgia, and Texas. Save room for the Georgia peach cobbler. *404 Ward Ave., Kaka'ako, tel. 808/596–8359. AE, D, DC, MC, V.*

Chinese

$ LEGENDS SEAFOOD RESTAURANT. When touring Chinatown, take time out and do dim sum for lunch. Here, you'll hear Chinese spoken as often as English. Try the prawn dumplings and fresh vegetables, and note the Hawaiian influence on the food in the form of deep-fried taro puffs. (Taro is the root from which poi is made.) *Chinese Cultural Plaza, 100 N. Beretania St., Downtown Honolulu, tel. 808/532–1868. AE, D, DC, MC, V.*

Contemporary

$$–$$$ CHEF MAVRO. Named for chef-owner George Mavrothalassitis,
★ formerly of the Four Seasons Maui and Halekūlani, this high-end bistro serves a fanciful fusion of French and Hawaiian cuisines. Signature dishes include baked *onaga* (red snapper) in a crust of Hawaiian salt, herbs, and *ogo* (seaweed), and the Hapūupūu bouillabaisse—Hawaiian sea bass, fisherman-style with aioli and

croutons. For dessert, the luscious lilikoi *malasadas* (passion-fruit-flavored Portuguese doughnut) are served with guava coulis and pineapple-coconut ice cream. Three prix-fixe menus are accompanied by suggested wines. The menu changes every six weeks, a testament to Chef Mavro's creativity and commitment to local ingredients. 1969 S. King St., Mōʻiliʻili, tel. 808/944–4714. *Reservations essential. AE, DC, MC, V. No lunch.*

$$–$$$ ALAN WONG'S. Chef-owner Alan Wong focuses heavily on
★ Hawaiian-grown products and he's utterly creative, turning local grinds into beautifully presented epicurean treats. For starters, get Da Bag, a puffed-up foil bag that's punctured at the table, revealing steamed clams, kālua pork, spinach, and shiitake mushrooms. Linger over macadamia nut–coconut crusted lamb chops or savor wasabi potato-crusted salmon. Don't miss the coconut sorbet served in a chocolate-and-macadamia-nut shell. The dining room itself is low-key, with a display kitchen. *McCully Court, 1857 S. King St., 3rd floor, Mōʻiliʻili, tel. 808/949–2526. AE, MC, V. No lunch.*

$$ HOKU'S AT THE KĀHALA MANDARIN ORIENTAL. Hoku's is earning raves and plenty of awards for its ambience, menu, and service. Here you can sample a world of cuisines from Indian nan bread baked in a tandoori oven to a wok-seared Maine lobster. The presentation is as innovative as the decor, which features a bamboo floor. The restaurant is on the lobby level of the hotel, front and center overlooking Kāhala Beach. *Kāhala Mandarin Oriental, 5000 Kāhala Ave., Kāhala, tel. 808/739–8780. AE, D, MC, V.*

$$ L'URAKU. If you like a little whimsy with your wasabi, then you'll appreciate the decor of this Japanese-European fusion restaurant, which stays sunny with its collection of bright, patterned umbrellas hanging from the ceiling. On the menu are almond-crusted snapper and a pan-roasted pork chop with crunchy shrimp. A prix-fixe menu is offered for $34. *1341 Kapiʻolani Blvd., Ala Moana, tel. 808/955–0552. AE, D, MC, V.*

$$ 3660 ON THE RISE. This casually stylish eatery is a 10-minute drive
★ from Waikīkī in the up-and-coming culinary mecca of Kaimukī.
Try the 'ahi katsu appetizer ('ahi wrapped in nori seaweed and deep-
fried medium rare with a wasabi-ginger sauce), fried oyster salad,
or Kalua duck risotto with grilled marinated shrimp. Love desserts?
Indulge in a warm chocolate soufflé cake or climb the mile-high
Waialae Pie, a blend of vanilla and coffee ice creams, macadamia
brittle, and caramel and chocolate sauces. A prix-fixe menu is also
available for $36. *3660 Waiʻalae Ave., Kaimuki, tel. 808/737–1177. AE,
DC, MC, V.*

$–$$ GORDON BIERSCH BREWERY RESTAURANT. Snuggling up to
★ Honolulu Harbor, this indoor-outdoor eatery, part of a West
Coast–based chain of microbreweries, is Aloha Tower
Marketplace's busiest. The menu is American with an island twist,
from Udon noodles with steamed clams and shiitake mushrooms
to a seafood Napoleon with crisp wontons and papaya salsa. You
can smell the garlic fries the moment you walk in. Ask for tastes
of the dark, medium, and light brews before choosing your
favorite. *Aloha Tower Marketplace, 1 Aloha Tower Dr., Downtown
Honolulu, tel. 808/599–4877. AE, D, DC, MC, V.*

$–$$ INDIGO. Indigo set the pace for a new generation of downtown
★ Honolulu eateries. The decor emphasizes wicker and track lighting,
and there's a charming back lānai that shields you from the
downtown hubbub. Owner Glenn Chu's variations on foods from
his Chinese heritage include crispy wontons stuffed with goat
cheese, Mongolian lamb chops, Szechuan peppered beef loin in
black bean sauce, and *bao* buns (steamed wheat-flour buns).
Don't forget to save room for Madame Pele's chocolate volcano
dessert. After dinner, check out Indigo's Green Room lounge next
door, ideal for sultry late-night jazz and a nightcap. *1121 Nuʻuanu
Ave., Downtown Honolulu, tel. 808/521–2900. AE, D, DC, MC, V.*

$–$$ ONJIN'S CAFE. Open for lunch only, Onjin's, across from Victoria
★ Ward Centre, is known for its fresh seafood dishes with a touch
of Asian influence, such as the crispy moi (threadfish) with ginger

and soy sauce or the almond-crusted soft-shell crab with citrus ponzu sauce (sweetened rice-wine-and-vinegar soy sauce). Orders for takeout dinners can be placed between 4 and 6 PM. *401 Kamakee St., Kaka'ako, tel. 808/589–1666. AE, D, MC, V. Closed weekends. No dinner.*

$–$$ **PALOMINO.** A downtown Honolulu favorite, this art deco Euro-
★ bistro, with handblown glass chandeliers, a grand staircase, and a 50-ft marble-and-mahogany bar, features a menu that fuses French, Spanish, and Italian cuisines. Entrées from the wood-burning oven include mahimahi with creamy polenta, fig-caper-olive relish, and mussels. Try the grilled ravioli for a change of pace. For seafood, consider the roasted prawns or shrimp in grape leaves. *Harbor Court, 66 Queen St., 3rd floor, Downtown Honolulu, tel. 808/528–2400. AE, D, DC, MC, V.*

$–$$ **SUNSET GRILL.** The sweet smell of wood smoke greets you as you enter the sleek Sunset Grill, which specializes in kiawe-broiled bistro cuisine. Choose from salmon cakes; kiawe-grilled ribs; or the salade niçoise, served with marinated grilled 'ahi and big enough for a whole dinner. The 20-oz kiawe-grilled Porterhouse steak is the dish here. Accompany your meal with a selection from the Grill's massive 800-selection wine list. *Restaurant Row, 500 Ala Moana Blvd., Downtown Honolulu, tel. 808/521–4409. AE, DC, MC, V.*

$ **KAKA'AKO KITCHEN.** If you want the culinary excellence of 3660 on the Rise with a downright casual island atmosphere, this is the place. Here, the owners of 3660 unleash their skills on the island-style "plate lunch." You can order your "two scoops rice" either white or brown. For vegetarians, the tofu burger is a superb choice. Better yet, order takeout and head across the street to Ala Moana Beach Park for a meal with a view. *Ward Centre, 1200 Ala Moana Blvd., Kaka'ako, tel. 808/596–7488. Reservations not accepted. No credit cards.*

German

$–$$ PATISSERIE. By day, this bakery in the Kāhala Mall is a deli, but five nights a week it turns into a 24-seat restaurant with great German food, a rarity in Hawai'i. The menu is small—only 10 entrées—but any choice is a good one. The Wiener schnitzel is juicy within its crispy crust, and veal ribs are garnished with a sprig of rosemary. Try the potato pancakes, crisp outside and soft inside, joined by a healthy spoonful of applesauce. The carrot salad is as delicious as the pastries. *Kāhala Mall, 4211 Wai'alae Ave., Kāhala, tel. 808/735–4402. Reservations not accepted. MC, V. Closed Sun.–Mon.*

Hawaiian

$$ THE WILLOWS. The outside of this restaurant gives little clue as to the wonderful ambience that awaits within its walls. Man-made ponds are sprinkled among the thatched dining pavilions, and you'll also find a tiny wedding chapel and a gallery gift shop. The food, served buffet-style, includes the trademark Willows' curry along with roasted Portobello mushrooms, *laulau* (a steamed bundle of ti leaves containing pork, butterfish, and taro tops), and pineapple-mango barbecued ribs. Willows, opened in 1944, has a reputation for historic Hawaiian hospitality. *901 Hausten St., Mō'ili'ili, tel. 808/952–9200. Reservations essential. AE, D, MC, V.*

$ 'ONO HAWAIIAN FOODS. The adventurous in search of a real "local food" experience should head to this no-frills hangout. You know it has to be good if residents are waiting in line to get in. Here you can sample poi, *lomi lomi salmon* (salmon massaged until tender and served with minced onions and tomatoes), laulau, kālua pork, and *haupia* (a light, gelatinlike dessert made from coconut). Appropriately enough, the Hawaiian word *'ono* means delicious. *726 Kapahulu Ave., Kapahulu, tel. 808/737–2275. Reservations not accepted. No credit cards. Closed Sun.*

Italian

$–$$ CAFE SISTINA. Sergio Mitrotti has gained quite a following with his inventive Italian-Mediterranean cuisine that is as artistic as the drawings on the café's walls. He's concocted an appetizer of goat cheese, chili peppers, garlic, prosciutto, and Greek olives, and he fills ravioli with such delights as Gorgonzola, porcini mushrooms, red peppers, and pancetta cream. Fresh chewy bread comes with a pesto butter to die for. *1314 S. King St., Makīkī, tel. 808/596–0061. AE, MC, V.*

Japanese

$–$$ SUSHI SASABUNE. This tiny sushi bar is the home of the island's most famous "trust me" sushi. Sit at the bar, and eat what the chef chooses for you. And don't expect a California roll. It might be something as exotic as teriyaki octopus. Sasabune's sushi specials also include crab, salmon, and tuna, and come with miso soup, seaweed salad, and adzuki-bean ice cream. The sushi is authentically Japanese, but created from such regional delicacies as Nova Scotia salmon and Louisanna blue crab. *1419 S. King St., Mōʻiliʻili, tel. 808/ 947–3800. Reservations essential. AE, D, DC, MC, V.*

Mexican

$–$$ COMPADRES MEXICAN BAR AND GRILL. The after-work crowd gathers here for potent margaritas and yummy pūpū. An outdoor terrace is best for cocktails and chips. Inside, the wooden floors, colorful photographs, and lively paintings create a festive setting for imaginative Mexican specialties. Fajitas, baby-back ribs, pork carnitas, and grilled shrimp are just a few of the many offerings. *Ward Centre, 1200 Ala Moana Blvd., Ala Moana, tel. 808/591–8307. D, MC, V.*

Eating Well is the Best Revenge

Eating out is a major part of every travel experience. It's a chance to explore flavors you don't find at home. And often the walking you do on vacation means that you can dig in without guilt.

START AT THE TOP By all means take in a really good restaurant or two while you're on the road. A trip is a time to kick back and savor the pleasures of the palate. Read up on the culinary scene before you leave home. Check out representative menus on the Web—some chefs have gone electronic. And ask friends who have just come back. Then reserve a table as far in advance as you can, remembering that the best establishments book up months in advance. Remember that some good restaurants require you to reconfirm the day before or the day of your meal. Then again, some really good places will call you, so make sure to leave a number where you can be reached.

ADVENTURES IN EATING A trip is the perfect opportunity to try food you can't get at home. So leave yourself open to try an ethnic food that's not represented where you live or to eat fruits and vegetables you've never heard of. One of them may become your next favorite food.

BEYOND GUIDEBOOKS You can rely on the restaurants you find in these pages. But also look for restaurants on your own. When you're ready for lunch, ask people you meet where they eat. Look for tiny holes-in-the-wall with a loyal following and the best burgers or crispiest pizza crust. Find out about local chains whose fame rests upon a single memorable dish. There's hardly a food-lover who doesn't relish the chance to share a favorite place. It's fun to come up with your own special find—and asking about food is a great way to start a conversation.

SAMPLE LOCAL FLAVORS Do check out the specialties. Is there a special brand of ice cream or a special dish that you simply must try?

HAVE A PICNIC Every so often eat al fresco. Grocery shopping gives you a whole different view of a place.

Seafood

$$-$$$ **SAM CHOY'S BREAKFAST, LUNCH AND CRAB & BIG ALOHA**
★ **BREWERY.** In this casual setting, great for families, diners can get
crackin' with crab, chow down on chowders, and fill up with an
abundance of both seafood and landlubber fare. This eatery's
warehouse size sets the tone for its large portions. An on-site
microbrewery brews eight varieties of Big Aloha beer. Sam Choy's
is located in Iwilei past downtown Honolulu on the highway
heading toward Honolulu International Airport. *580 Nimitz Hwy.,
Iwilei, tel. 808/545–7979.* AE, D, DC, MC, V.

Steak

$$-$$$ **RUTH'S CHRIS STEAK HOUSE.** This pastel-hue dining room on
Restaurant Row may not look like the typical steak house, but it
has all the prerequisites: USDA prime corn-fed Midwestern beef,
large portions, and generous side orders, including a creamy
spinach au gratin. Charbroiled fish, veal, and lamb chops provide
nice alternatives to the steaks. For dessert, try the house special,
a bread pudding soaked in whiskey sauce. *Restaurant Row, 500 Ala
Moana Ave., Downtown Honolulu, tel. 808/599–3860 or 800/544–
0808.* AE, DC, MC, V.

In This Chapter

Updated by Maggie Wunsch

shopping

HONOLULU IS THE NUMBER-ONE SHOPPING SPOT in the Islands and an international crossroads of the shopping scene. It has sprawling shopping malls, unique boutiques, hotel arcades, neighborhood businesses, and a variety of other enterprises. Major shopping malls are generally open daily from 10 to 9; smaller neighborhood boutiques are usually 9-to-5 operations.

SHOPPING CENTERS

In Honolulu

Ala Moana Shopping Center (1450 Ala Moana Blvd., Ala Moana, tel. 808/955–9517 for special-events information and information about shuttle service) is one of the nation's largest open-air malls and just five minutes from Waikīkī by bus. More than 200 stores, restaurants, and services make up this 50-acre complex. All of Hawai'i's major department stores are here, including Neiman Marcus, Sears, JCPenney, and Macy's. Palm Boulevard features upscale designer fashions, such as Gucci, Louis Vuitton, Gianni Versace, and Emporio Armani.

Aloha Tower Marketplace (1 Aloha Tower Dr., at Piers 8, 9, and 10, Downtown Honolulu, tel. 808/566–2337, www.alohatower. com/atm for special-events information) cozies up to Honolulu Harbor and bills itself as a festival marketplace. Along with restaurants and entertainment venues, it has 80 shops and kiosks selling mostly visitor-oriented merchandise, from expensive sunglasses to souvenir refrigerator magnets.

DFS Galleria Waikīkī (corner of Kalākaua and Royal Hawaiian Aves., Waikīkī, tel. 808/931–2655) has boutiques of world-class designers—such as Hermès, Cartier, and Calvin Klein—as well as Hawai'i's largest beauty and cosmetic store. An "Old Hawai'i" atmosphere is created by a three-story replica of a 1920s luxury cruise liner; daily Hawaiian music and dance performances; and the Waikīkī Walk, with authentic fashions, arts and crafts, and gifts of the Hawaiian Islands. There is also an exclusive boutique floor available to duty-free shoppers only. The Kalia Grill and Starbucks offers a respite for weary shoppers.

Kāhala Mall (4211 Wai'alae Ave., Kāhala, tel. 808/732–7736) has 90 retail outlets including Macy's, The Gap, Reyn's Aloha Wear, and Barnes & Noble. Restaurants range from quick-bite venues to leisurely meal places. Kāhala Mall's Main Stage spotlights entertaining weekend arts performances ranging from local ballet to contemporary Hawaiian music concerts weekends and evenings. Along with an assortment of gift shops, Kāhala Mall also has eight movie theaters (tel. 808/733–6233) for post-shopping entertainment. The mall is 10 minutes by car from Waikīkī in the chic residential neighborhood of Kāhala, near the slopes of Diamond Head.

The fashionable **King Kalākaua Plaza** (2080 Kalākaua Ave., Waikīkī, tel. 808/955–2878), one of Waikīkī's newer shopping destinations, offers flagship stores Banana Republic and Nike Town as well as the All Sports Hawaii Cafe.

The **Royal Hawaiian Shopping Center** (2201 Kalākaua Ave., Waikīkī, tel. 808/922–0588, www.shopwaikiki.com), fronting the Royal Hawaiian and Sheraton Waikīkī hotels, is three blocks long and contains 150 stores on four levels. There are upscale establishments such as Chanel and Cartier, as well as the Hawaiian Heirloom Jewelry Collection by Philip Rickard, which also has a museum with Victorian jewelry pieces. Bike buffs can check out the Harley-Davidson MotorClothes and Collectibles Boutique. The center has 15 restaurants, including the Paradiso Seafood Grill and Villa Paradiso, and even has a post office.

Heading west from Waikīkī toward downtown Honolulu, you'll run into a section of town with five distinct shopping-complex areas known as the **Victoria Ward Centers**; there are more than 100 specialty shops and 17 restaurants here. The Ward 16 Entertainment Complex features 16 movie theaters and a Shopping Concierge to assist you in navigating your way through the center's five complexes. Two of the largest and most popular are Ward Warehouse (1050 Ala Moana Blvd., Ala Moana) and Ward Centre (1200 Ala Moana Blvd., Ala Moana).

Waikīkī Shopping Plaza (2270 Kalākaua Ave., Waikīkī, tel. 808/ 923–1111) is across the street from the Royal Hawaiian Shopping Center. Its landmark is a 75-ft-high water-sculpture gizmo, which looks great when it's working. Walden Books, Guess, Clio Blue jewelers, and Tanaka of Tokyo Restaurant are some of the 50 shops and restaurants on six floors.

Waikīkī has three theme park–style shopping centers. Right in the heart of the area is the **International Market Place** (2330 Kalākaua Ave., Waikīkī, tel. 808/971–2080), a tangle of 150 souvenir shops and stalls under a giant banyan tree. **Waikīkī Town Center** (2301 Kūhiō Ave., Waikīkī, tel. 808/922–2724) is an open-air complex with a variety of shops ranging from fashions to jewelry. There are free hula shows here Monday, Wednesday, Friday, and Saturday at 7 PM. **King's Village** (131 Kaʻiulani Ave., Waikīkī, tel. 808/944–6855) looks like a Hollywood stage set of monarchy-era Honolulu, complete with a changing-of-the-guard ceremony every evening at 6:15; shops include Hawaiian Island Creations Jewelry, Swim City USA Swimwear, and Island Motor Sports.

Around the Island

Aloha Flea Market (99-500 Salt Lake Blvd., 'Aiea, tel. 808/732–9611 or 808/486–1529) is a thrice-weekly outdoor bazaar that attracts hundreds of vendors and even more bargain hunters. Operations range from slick tents with rows of neatly stacked, new merchandise to garage-sale treasures. Every Hawaiian souvenir imaginable can be found here, from coral shell necklaces to bikinis, to a variety of ethnic wares from Chinese brocade dresses to Japanese pottery. The flea market takes place in the Aloha Stadium parking lot Wednesday and weekends from 6 to 3; the $6 admission fee includes round-trip shuttle service from Waikīkī.

The **Waikele Premium Outlets** (H-1 Fwy., Waikele, 30 minutes west of downtown Honolulu, Waikele, tel. 808/676–5656) reflects Hawai'i's latest craze: manufacturer-direct shopping at discount prices. Among its tenants are the Anne Klein Factory, Donna Karan Company Store, Kenneth Cole, and Saks Fifth Avenue Outlet.

SPECIALTY STORES

Clothing

HIGH FASHION

Neiman Marcus (Ala Moana Shopping Center, 1450 Ala Moana Blvd., Ala Moana, tel. 808/951–8887) is the trendy end of the high-fashion scene. For the latest in footwear, **Nordstrom Shoes** (Ala Moana Shopping Center, 1450 Ala Moana Blvd., Ala Moana, tel. 808/973–4620) displays an elegant array of pricey styles. Top-of-the-line international fashions for men and women are available at **Mandalay Imports** (Halekūlani, 2199 Kālia Rd., Waikīkī, tel. 808/922–7766), home of Star of Siam silks and cottons, Anne Namba couture, and designs by Choisy, who works out of Bangkok. **Pzazz** (1419 Kalākaua Ave., Waikīkī, tel. 808/955–5800), nicknamed the Ann Taylor of consignment shops, sells high fashion at low prices.

ISLAND WEAR

For stylish Hawaiian wear, the kind worn by local men and women, look in one of the **Macy's** branches at Ala Moana Shopping Center, Kāhala Mall, or in downtown Honolulu (1450 Ala Moana Blvd., Ala Moana, tel. 808/941–2345 for all stores). **Native Books and Beautiful Things** (Ward Warehouse, 1050 Ala Moana Blvd., Downtown Honolulu, tel. 808/537–2926) sells hand-painted, one-of-a-kind clothing created by local artisans. **Ohelo Road** (Kāhala Mall, 4211 Wai'alae Ave., Kāhala, tel. 808/735–5525) carries island print dresses in materials that make living in the tropics cool year-round. For menswear and select women's and children's alohawear, try **Reyn's** (Ala Moana Shopping Center, 1450 Ala Moana Blvd., Ala Moana, tel. 808/949–5929; Kāhala Mall, 4211 Wai'alae Ave., Kāhala, tel. 808/737–8313; Sheraton Waikīkī, 2255 Kalākaua Ave., Waikīkī, tel. 808/923–0331).

If you're looking for alohawear that ranges from the bright-and-bold to the cool-and-classy, try **Hilo Hattie** (700 N. Nimitz Hwy., Iwilei, tel. 808/537–2926), the world's largest manufacturer of Hawaiian and tropical fashions; it's also a good source for island souvenirs. Free shuttle service is available from Waikīkī. For vintage aloha shirts, try **Bailey's Antique Clothing and Thrift Shop** (517 Kapahulu Ave., tel. 808/734–7628), on the edge of Waikīkī.

Gifts

Following Sea (Kāhala Mall, 4211 Wai'alae Ave., Kāhala, tel. 808/734–4425) sells beautiful handmade jewelry and pottery.

To send home tropical flowers, contact **Hawaiian Greenhouse** (tel. 888/965–8351, www.hawaiiangreenhouse.com). **Robyn Buntin Galleries** (820 S. Beretania St., Honolulu, tel. 808/545–

5572) presents Chinese nephrite jade carvings, Japanese lacquer and screens, Buddhist sculptures, and other international pieces. **Takenoya Arts** (Halekūlani, 2199 Kālia Rd., Waikīkī, tel. 808/926–1939) specializes in intricately carved netsuke (toggles used to fasten containers to kimonos), both antique and contemporary, and one-of-a-kind necklaces.

Hawaiian Arts and Crafts

Items handcrafted of native Hawaiian wood make lovely gifts. Koa and milo each have a beautiful color and grain. The great koa forests are disappearing because of environmental factors, so the wood is becoming valuable; most koa products you'll encounter are produced from wood grown on commercial farms.

A wonderful selection of Hawaiian arts, crafts, and children's toys can be found at **My Little Secret** (Ward Warehouse, 1050 Ala Moana Blvd., tel. 808/596–2990).

For hula costumes and instruments, try **Hula Supply Center** (2346 S. King St. Mō'ili'ili, tel. 808/941–5379). You can purchase traditional island comforters, wall hangings, pillows, and other Hawaiian quilt print items at **Hawaiian Quilt Collection** (Ala Moana Center, 1450 Ala Moana Blvd., Ala Moana, tel. 808/946–2233). For high-end collector's items, head to **Martin & MacArthur** (Aloha Tower Marketplace, 1 Aloha Tower Dr., Downtown Honolulu, tel. 808/524–6066), specialists in items made from the Hawaiian koa wood, including desk accessories, frames, jewelry, hand mirrors, and handcrafted furniture.

Jewelry

Bernard Hurtig's (Hilton Hawaiian Village Ali'i Tower, 2005 Kālia Rd., Waikīkī, tel. 808/947–9399) sells fine jewelry with an emphasis on 18-karat gold and antique jade. **Haimoff & Haimoff Creations in Gold** (Halekūlani, 2199 Kālia Rd.,

Waikīkī, tel. 808/923–8777) sells the work of jewelry designer Harry Haimoff.

Coral and pearl jewelry is popular, stunning, and fairly affordable. To see where it comes from and how jewelry is designed using these treasures from the sea, take a tour of the **Maui Divers Jewelry Design Center** (1520 Liona St., Mōʻiliʻili, Honolulu, tel. 808/943–8383).

In This Chapter

Updated by Maggie Wunsch

outdoor activities and sports

WHETHER YOU SOAR ABOVE THEM, sail on them, or dive into them, the waters surrounding Oʻahu are an ocean lover's dream. The seas off Waikīkī call to novices looking for a surfing lesson and outrigger canoe ride, while the North Shore beckons accomplished wave riders. Snorkeling and scuba diving at Hanauma Bay, on the island's eastern tip, bring you face-to-face with a rainbow of sea creatures. Honolulu's Kewalo Basin is the starting point for most fishing charters and the Honolulu harborfront piers serve as home port for many luxury cruise excursions. Windsurfers and ocean kayakers head to the beaches of the windward side, Lanikai in particular. Oʻahu offers a bounty of land activities as well: hiking, rock-climbing, horseback riding, golf, tennis, and biking, to name a few.

BEACHES

For South Seas sun, fun, and surf, Oʻahu is a dream destination, but first some words of caution: when approaching any Hawaiian beach, heed signs indicating current surf conditions. If they warn of dangerous surf or currents, pay attention. Most beaches have lifeguards, although two exceptions are Kahana and Mālaekahano. Waikīkī is only 21 degrees north of the equator, so the sun here is very strong. No alcoholic beverages are allowed, and no matter which beach you choose, lock your car and never, ever leave your valuables unattended.

Waikīkī Beaches

The 2½-mi strand called **Waikīkī Beach** actually extends from Hilton Hawaiian Village on one end to Kapiʻolani Park and Diamond Head on the other. Areas along this sandy strip have separate names but subtle differences. Beach areas are listed here from west to east.

★ **KAHANAMOKU BEACH.** Named for Hawaiʻi's famous Olympic swimming champion, Duke Kahanamoku, this beach has decent snorkeling and swimming and a gentle surf. Its sandy bottom slopes gradually. The area has a snack concession, showers, a beach-gear and surfboard rental shop, catamaran cruises, and a sand volleyball court. *In front of Hilton Hawaiian Village Beach Resort and Spa.*

★ **FT. DERUSSY BEACH.** Sunbathers, swimmers, and windsurfers enjoy this beach, one of the widest in Waikīkī, fronting the military hotel, the Hale Koa, and the U.S. Army Museum. It trails off to a coral ocean bottom with fairly good snorkeling sights. There are volleyball courts, food stands, picnic tables, dressing rooms, and showers. *In front of Ft. DeRussy and Hale Koa Hotel.*

GRAY'S BEACH. Named for a little lodging house called Gray's-by-the-Sea, which stood here in the 1920s, this beach is known for two good surfing spots called Paradise and Number Threes just beyond its reef. High tides often cover the narrow beach. *In front of Halekūlani.*

★ **KAHALOA AND ULUKOU BEACHES.** Possibly the best swimming and lots of activities are available along this little stretch of Waikīkī Beach. Take a catamaran or outrigger canoe ride out into the bay, unless you're ready to try your skill at surfing. *In front of Royal Hawaiian Hotel and Sheraton Moana Surfrider.*

★ **KŪHIŌ BEACH PARK.** This beach is a hot spot for shoreline and beach activities. Check out the Kūhiō Beach stage nightly at 6:30

for free hula and Hawaiian-music performances; weekends there's a torchlighting ceremony at sunset as well. Surf lessons for beginners are available from the beach center here every half hour. *Past the Sheraton Moana Surfrider Hotel to Kapahulu Ave. pier.*

QUEEN'S SURF. A great place for a sunset picnic, this beach is beyond the seawall, toward Diamond Head, at what's known as the "other end of Waikīkī." It was once the site of Queen Lili'uokalani's beach house. A mix of families and gay couples gather here, and it seems as if someone is always playing a steel drum. There are good shade trees, picnic tables, and a changing house with showers. *Across from entrance to Honolulu Zoo.*

SANS SOUCI. Nicknamed Dig-Me Beach because of its outlandish display of skimpy bathing suits, this small rectangle of sand is nonetheless a good sunning spot for all ages. Children enjoy its shallow, safe waters, and the shore draws many ocean kayakers and outrigger canoeists. Serious swimmers and triathletes also swim in the channel here, beyond the reef. There's no food concession, but near one end is the Hau Tree Lānai restaurant. *Makai side of Kapi'olani Park, between New Otani Kaimana Beach Hotel and Waikīkī War Memorial Natatorium.*

DIAMOND HEAD BEACH. This narrow strip of beach is not good for swimmers due to the reef just offshore, but it's still a great spot for watching windsurfers and wave boarders strut their skills across the water. Parking is located on Diamond Head Road, just past the Diamond Head Lighthouse. From the parking area, look for an opening in the makai wall where an unpaved trail leads down to the beach.

Beaches Around O'ahu

★ **HANAUMA BAY.** The main attraction here is snorkeling. The coral reefs are clearly visible through the turquoise waters of this sunken volcanic crater half open to the ocean. It is a designated marine preserve and features a marine life education center for visitors. Although the fish are the tamest you'll view while snorkeling, feeding them is not allowed. The bay is best early in the morning (around 7), before the crowds arrive. It can be difficult to park later in the day. There is a busy food and snorkel-equipment concession on the beach, plus changing rooms and showers. No smoking is allowed, and the beach is closed on Tuesday. **Hanauma Bay Snorkeling Excursions** (tel. 808/373–5060) run to and from Waikīkī. *7455 Kalaniana'ole Hwy., tel. 808/ 396–4229. Donation $3; parking $1; mask, snorkel, and fins rental $6. Wed.–Mon. 6–6.*

SANDY BEACH. Strong, steady winds make "Sandy's" a kite-flyer's paradise. There's a changing house with indoor and outdoor showers but no food concessions. Unless you are an expert at navigating rip currents and very shallow shore breaks, this beach is dangerous for the casual swimmer—more neck and spine injuries occur here than anywhere else on the island. *Makai of Kalaniana'ole Hwy., 2 mi east of Hanauma Bay.*

MAKAPU'U BEACH. Swimming at Makapu'u should be attempted only by strong strokers and bodysurfers, because the swells can be overwhelmingly big and powerful. Instead, consider this tiny crescent cove—popular with locals—as a prime sunbathing spot. Finding parking in the small lot can be tricky. In a pinch, try parking on the narrow shoulder and walking down to the beach. There is a changing house with indoor and outdoor showers. *Makai of Kalaniana'ole Hwy., across from Sea Life Park, 2 mi south of Waimānalo.*

★ **WAIMĀNALO BEACH PARK.** This is a "local" beach busy with picnicking families and active sports fields. Sometimes, folks are not very friendly to tourists here, and there have been some incidents of car theft, but the beach itself is one of the island's most beautiful. Expect a wide stretch of sand; turquoise, emerald, and deep-blue seas; and waves full of boogie boarders. *Windward side, look for signs makai of Kalaniana'ole Hwy., south of Waimānalo town.*

BELLOWS BEACH. The waves here are great for bodysurfing. Locals come for the fine swimming on weekends and holidays, when the Air Force opens the beach to civilians. There are showers, abundant parking, and plenty of spots for picnicking underneath shady ironwood trees. There is no food concession, but McDonald's and other take-out fare is available right outside the entrance gate. *Entrance on Kalaniana'ole Hwy. near Waimānalo town center, signs on makai side of road.*

★ **KAILUA BEACH PARK.** Steady breezes attract windsurfers by the dozens to this long, palm-fringed beach with gently sloping sands. You can rent equipment in Kailua and try it yourself. This is a local favorite, so if you want the beach to yourself, head here on a weekday. There are showers, changing rooms, picnic areas, and a concession stand. Buy your picnic provisions at the Kalapawai Market nearby. *Windward side, makai of Kailua town, turn right on Kailua Rd. at market, cross bridge, then turn left into beach parking lot.*

LANIKAI BEACH PARK. A mile of buttery sand ideal for a beach stroll, with views of water the color of turquoise. The beach fronts some of the most expensive real estate on the windward side. When the trade winds are active, look for windsurfers. Early birds can watch some spectacular sunrises. *Windward side, past Kailua Beach Park, street parking on Mokulua Dr. for various public access points to beach.*

KAHANA BAY BEACH PARK. Local parents often bring their children to wade in safety at this pretty beach cove with very shallow, protected waters. A grove of tall ironwood and pandanus trees keeps the area cool, shady, and ideal for a picnic. An ancient Hawaiian fishpond, which was in use until the '20s, is visible nearby. There are changing houses, showers, and picnic tables. *Windward side of island, makai of Kamehameha Hwy., north of Kualoa Park.*

KUALOA REGIONAL PARK. This is one of the island's most beautiful picnic, camping, and beach areas. Grassy expanses border a long, narrow stretch of beach with spectacular views of Kāneʻohe Bay and the Koʻolau Mountains. Dominating the view is an islet called Mokoliʻi, which rises 206 ft above the water. You can swim in the shallow areas year-round. The one drawback is that it's usually windy. Bring a cooler because no refreshments are sold here. There are places to shower, change, and picnic in the shade of palm trees. *Windward side, makai of Kamehameha Hwy., north of Waiāhole.*

MĀLAEKAHANA BEACH PARK. The big attraction here is tiny Goat Island, a bird sanctuary just offshore. At low tide the water is shallow enough—never more than waist high—so that you can wade out to it. Wear sneakers so you don't cut yourself on the coral. Families love to camp in the groves of ironwood trees at Mālaekahana State Park. The beach itself is fairly narrow but long enough for a 20-minute stroll, one-way. The waves are never too big, and sometimes they're just right for the beginning bodysurfer. There are changing houses, showers, and picnic tables. Note that the entrance gates are easy to miss because you can't see the beach from the road. *Windward side, entrance gates are makai of Kamehameha Hwy., ½ mi north of Lāʻie.*

SUNSET BEACH. This is one link in the chain of North Shore beaches that extends for miles. It's popular for its gentle summer waves and crashing winter surf. The beach is broad, and the sand is soft. Lining the adjacent highway there are usually carryout truck stands selling shaved ice, plate lunches, and sodas. *North Shore, 1 mi north of ʻEhukai Beach Park on makai side of Kamehameha Hwy.*

ʻEHUKAI BEACH PARK. ʻEhukai is part of a series of beaches running for many miles along the North Shore. What sets it apart is the view of the famous Banzai Pipeline, where the waves curl into magnificent tubes, making it an experienced wave-rider's dream. In spring and summer, the waves are more accommodating to the average swimmer. The long, wide, and generally uncrowded beach has a changing house with toilets and an outdoor shower. Bring along drinks because there is very little shade here, and the nearest store is a mile away. *North Shore, 1 mi north of Foodland store at Pūpūkea, turn makai off Kamehameha Hwy. directly into the small parking lot bordering highway.*

★ **WAIMEA BAY.** Made popular in that old Beach Boys song "Surfin' U.S.A.," Waimea Bay is a slice of hang-ten heaven and home to the king-size 25- to 30-ft winter waves. Summer is the time to swim and snorkel in the calm waters. The beach is a broad crescent of soft sand backed by a shady area with tables, a changing house, and showers. Parking is almost impossible in the lot on weekends, so folks just park along the road and walk down. *North Shore across from Waimea Valley, 3 mi north of Hale'iwa on makai side of Kamehameha Hwy.*

HALE'IWA ALI'I BEACH PARK. The winter waves are impressive here, but in summer the ocean is like a lake, ideal for family swimming. The beach itself is big and often full of locals. Its broad lawns off the highway invite volleyball and Frisbee games and groups of barbecuers. There is a changing house with showers but no food concessions. Hale'iwa has everything you need for provisions. *North Shore, makai side of Kamehameha Hwy., north of Hale'iwa town center and past harbor.*

YOKOHAMA BAY. You'll be one of the few outsiders at this Wai'anae Coast beach at the very end of the road. It feels and looks remote and untouched, which may explain the lack of crowds. Locals come here to fish and swim in waters that are calm enough for children in summer. The beach is narrow and rocky in places. Bring provisions, because the nearest town is a 15-minute drive away. There's a changing house and showers, plus a small parking lot, but most folks just pull over and park on the side of the bumpy road. *Wai'anae Coast, northern end of Farrington Hwy. about 7 mi north of Mākaha.*

MĀKAHA BEACH PARK. This beach provides a slice of local life most visitors don't see. Families string up tarps for the day, fire up hibachis, set up lawn chairs, get out the fishing gear, and strum 'ukuleles while they "talk story" (chat). The swimming is generally decent in the summer, but avoid the big winter waves. This was home to the island's first professional surf meet, in 1952. The ¼-mi beach has a changing house and showers and is the site of a yearly big-board surf meet. *Wai'anae Coast, 1½ hrs west of Honolulu on H-1 Fwy. and Farrington Hwy., makai side of hwy.*

★ **ALA MOANA BEACH PARK.** Ala Moana has a protective reef, which keeps the waters calm and perfect for swimming. After Waikīkī, this is the most popular beach among visitors. To the Waikīkī side is a peninsula called Magic Island, with picnic tables, shady trees, and paved sidewalks ideal for jogging. Ala Moana also has playing fields, changing houses, indoor and outdoor showers, lifeguards, concession stands, and tennis courts. This beach is for everyone, but only in the daytime. It's a high-crime area after dark. *Honolulu, makai side of Ala Moana Shopping Center and Ala Moana Blvd.; from Waikīkī take Bus 8 to shopping center and cross Ala Moana Blvd.*

PARTICIPANT SPORTS

Biking

Coastal roads are flat and well paved. On the downside, they're also awash in vehicular traffic. Frankly, biking is no fun in either Waikīkī or Honolulu, but things are a bit better outside the city. Be sure to take along a nylon jacket for the frequent showers on the windward side and remember that Hawai'i is Paradise after the Fall: lock up your bike.

Mountain bikes are available for rent at **Blue Sky Rentals & Sports Center** (1920 Ala Moana Blvd., across from the Hilton Hawaiian Village, Waikīkī, tel. 808/947–0101). Rates are $15 a day (from 8 to 6), $20 for 24 hours, and $75 per week, plus a $25 deposit. This price includes a bike, a helmet, a lock, and a water bottle.

If you want to find some biking buddies, write ahead to the **Hawai'i Bicycling League** (Box 4403, Honolulu 96813, tel. 808/735–5756, www.bikehawaii.com), which can tell you about upcoming races and club rides (frequent on all the Islands).

For biking information and maps, contact the **Honolulu City and County Bike Coordinator** (tel. 808/527–5044).

Tour O'ahu's North Shore by bike with guided tours from **Waimea Falls Park** (59-864 Kamehameha Hwy., Hale'iwa, tel. 808/638–8511). Admission to the park is $24, with additional charges based on activity package chosen.

Camping and Hiking

For a free O'ahu recreation map that outlines the island's 33 major trails, including the visitor-friendly Mānoa Falls Trail, Makapu'u Lighthouse Trail, Wa'ahila Ridge Trail, and Leeward's O'ahu's Kaena Point, contact the **Hawai'i State Department of Land and Natural Resources** (1151 Punchbowl St., Room 130, Downtown Honolulu, Honolulu 96813, tel. 808/587–030, www.hawaii.gov).

For a complimentary hiking safety guide, contact the City and County of Honolulu's **Trails and Access Manager** (tel. 808/973–9782). Ask for a copy of "Hiking on O'ahu: The Official Guide."

For families, the **Hawai'i Nature Center** (2131 Makiki Heights Dr., Makiki Heights, Honolulu, 96822, tel. 808/955–0100) in upper Makiki Valley conducts a number of programs for both adults and children. The center conducts guided hikes into tropical settings that reveal hidden waterfalls and protected forest reserves. **O'ahu Nature Tours** (tel. 808/924–2473 or 800/861–6018, www.oahunaturetours.com) offers glorious sunrise, rain-forest, and volcanic walking tours with an escort who will explain the wealth of native flora and fauna that is your companion along the way.

Camping on O'ahu is available at four state parks, 12 county beach parks, and within the grounds of one county botanic garden. Stays are restricted to five nights per month in all beach and state recreation areas, and parks are closed to campers on Wednesday and Thursday evenings. To obtain a free camping permit for state parks, write to **Department of Land and Natural Resources, State Parks Division** (Box 621, Honolulu, 96809, tel. 808/587–0300). For county and beach parks, contact the **Honolulu Department of Parks and Recreation** (650 S. King St., Honolulu 96813, tel. 808/523–4525). A word of caution: although some O'ahu recreation areas have caretakers and gates that close in the evening for your safety, many others can be quite isolated at night.

Mālaekahana State Park on the North Shore is a local favorite camping spot and offers a beachfront setting with two areas that include rest rooms, showers, picnic tables, and drinking water. It's on Kamehameha Highway between Lā'ie and Kahuku. On the windward coast, **Ho'omaluhia Botanic Gardens,** (45-680 Luluku Rd., Kaneohe, tel. 808/523–4525) provides a safe, scenic camping setting at the base of the majestic Ko'olau Mountains. Five grassy camping areas with rest rooms, showers, and drinking water are available on Friday, Saturday, and Sunday evenings only. Permits are free and are issued at the garden daily between 9 and 4.

You can rent everything from tents to backpacks at **The Bike Shop** (1149 S. King St., Mō'ili'ili, Honolulu, tel. 808/595–0588).

Fitness Centers and Spas

HONOLULU

Abhasa Spa. Cold laser anti-aging treatments, vegetarian lifestyle–spa therapies, color-light therapy, and body cocooning are all available here in this spa tucked away in the Royal Hawaiian Hotel's coconut grove. *Royal Hawaiian Hotel, 2259 Kalākaua Ave., Waikīkī, tel. 808/922–8200.*

Ampy's European Facials and Body Spa. This spa is famous for its European-style facials; massages; and day spa packages, including a Gentlemen's Retreat. It's located in the Ala Moana Building, adjacent to Ala Moana Shopping Center. *1441 Kapiolani Blvd., Ala Moana, tel. 808/946–3838.*

Clark Hatch Physical Fitness Center. Weight-training facilities, an indoor pool, a racquetball court, aerobics classes, and treadmills are all available at this club. *745 Fort St., Downtown Honolulu, tel. 808/536–7205. About $10 per day. Weekdays 6 AM–8 PM, Sat. 7:30–5:30.*

Hawaiian Rainforest Salon and Spa. Vichy showers; a sauna; facial and massage treatments; and complete hair, nail, and makeup services are available here. *Pacific Beach Hotel, 5th floor, 2490 Kalākaua Ave., Waikīkī, tel. 808/922–1233.*

Malama Salon Spas. Malama has two locations, one on the third level of Ala Moana Shopping Center adjacent to Neiman Marcus, and the other in Mānoa Valley, about 15 minutes from Waikīkī. These Aveda Lifestyle Salons offer massages, facials, and body and beauty treatments in settings so serene and elegant you may forget just how busy the world is outside the front doors. *Ala Moana Shopping Center, 3rd level, 1450 Ala Moana Blvd., Ala Moana; 2801 E. Mānoa Rd., Honolulu, tel. 808/988–0101 for both locations.*

Mandara Spa and Holistica Hawaii Wellness Center. This 42,000-square-ft spa and wellness center spans two floors of the Hilton Hawaiian Village's Kalia Tower. You'll find a cardiovascular fitness center, outdoor lānai and spa suites, and a wealth of spa treatments and salon services that incorporate Hawaiian, Asian, European, and Polynesian techniques. Holistica Hawaii will guide you in your quest for a healthy lifestyle. *Hilton Hawaiian Village, 2005 Kālia Rd., Waikīkī, tel. 808/949–4321.*

Na Ho'ola at the Hyatt Waikīkī. Come here for an authentic Hawaiian spa experience with poolside lomi lomi (Hawaiian massage), Reiki treatments, ti leaf and Polynesian aloe body wraps, thalasso therapies, and fitness facilities with cardio-workout equipment. *2424 Kalākaua Ave., Waikīkī, tel. 808/921–6097.*

Paul Brown Salon and Day Spa. Indulge in a tropical-fruit facial or mineral body wrap followed by an aromatherapy massage. Paul Brown offers spa pampering and complete hair-salon services. *Ward Centre, 1200 Ala Moana Blvd., Ala Moana, tel. 808/591–1881.*

Serenity Spa Hawai'i. Aromatherapy treatments, massages, and facials are provided in an atmosphere of serene calm, only steps off the beach. *Outrigger Reef on the Beach, 2169 Kalia Rd., Waikīkī, tel. 808/926–2882.*

24-Hour Fitness. Waikīkī's most accessible fitness center has weight-training machines, cardiovascular equipment, free weights, and a pro shop. *Pacific Beach Hotel, 2nd floor, 2490 Kalākaua Ave., Waikīkī, tel. 808/971–4653. $10 per day for guests of many Waikīkī hotels (call for list), $20 for nonguests. Daily.*

AROUND THE ISLAND

'Ihilani Resort & Spa. About 25 minutes from the airport is O'ahu's largest health and fitness center. There's 35,000 square ft of space for classes, weight rooms, relaxation programs, hydrotherapies—you name it. Call for prices and to arrange nonguest privileges. *J. W. Marriott 'Ihilani Resort & Spa, 92-1001 Olani St., Kapolei, tel. 808/679–0079.*

Golf

O'ahu has more than three dozen public and private golf courses. Hotel concierges can assist with tee times and transportation. To get a preview before you arrive, check out www.808golf.com, which offers a comprehensive on-line guide to Hawai'i golf, including course descriptions and tee-time reservations. For last-minute tee times, consult Standby Golf at 888/645-2665. Standby Golf has access to 39 courses on Oahu and it is possible to book some courses a full day ahead of time at reasonable rates.

Ala Wai Golf Course. One of the most popular municipal 18-hole courses is on Waikīkī's mauka end, across the Ala Wai Canal. It's par 70 on 6,424 yards and has a pro shop and a restaurant. There's always a waiting list for tee times, so if you plan to play, call the minute you land. *404 Kapahulu Ave., Waikīkī, tel. 808/733-7387. Greens fee $42; cart $14.*

Coral Creek Golf Course. A new addition to the Ewa Beach plains, this 18-hole, 6,808-yd, par-72 course offers wind challenges, ravines, coral rock formations, and lakes. *91-1111 Geiger Rd., 'Ewa Beach, tel. 808/441-4653. Greens fee $135, cart included.*

Hawai'i Kai Championship Course. Advance reservations are recommended at this 18-hole, 6,222-yard course and the neighboring 18-hole, 2,386-yard Hawai'i Kai Executive Course. *8902 Kalaniana'ole Hwy., Hawai'i Kai, Honolulu, tel. 808/395-2358, www.hawaiikaigolf.com. Greens fee weekdays $90 for Championship Course and $37 for Executive Course; weekends and holidays $100 and $42, respectively; cart included.*

Hawai'i Prince Golf Club. This 27-hole Arnold Palmer–designed course welcomes visiting players. *91-1200 Ft. Weaver Rd., 'Ewa Beach, tel. 808/944-4567. Greens fee $90 guests, $135 nonguests; cart included.*

Kahuku Golf Course. The 9-hole walking-only course is played more by locals than by visitors, but serves up some stunning North Shore natural beauty. *56-501 Kamehameha Hwy., Kahuku, tel. 808/293–5842. Greens fee $20 for nonresidents; hand cart rental $4.*

Ko Olina Golf Club. Affiliated with the 'Ihilani Resort is this club on O'ahu's west side. Its 18 holes are beautifully landscaped with waterfalls and ponds where black and white swans serve as your gallery. *Ko Olina Resort, 92-1220 Ali'inui Dr., Kapolei, tel. 808/676–5300, www.koolinagolf.com. Greens fee $145, cart included.*

Ko'olau Golf Club. This 18-hole, par-72 course on O'ahu's windward side in Kaneohe is officially rated by the United States Golf Association as the most difficult golf course in the country. Up for the challenge? *45-550 Kionaole Rd., Kaneohe, tel. 808/236–0005. Greens fee $100, cart included.*

Links at Kuilima at Turtle Bay Resort. The 18 holes here were designed by Arnold Palmer and Ed Seay around Punahoolapa Marsh, a protected wetland for endangered Hawaiian waterfowl. The 9-hole George Fazio Course is being expanded to 18 holes and is scheduled, at press time, to open in winter 2002. *Turtle Bay Resort, 57-091 Kamehameha Hwy., Kahuku, tel. 808/293–8574. Greens fee $75 guests, $125 nonguests; cart included.*

Luana Hills Country Club. The front nine of this 18-hole, par-72 course is carved in the slopes of Mount Olomana. *770 Auloa Rd., Kailua, tel. 808/262–2139. Greens fee $95, cart included.*

Mililani Golf Club. The tree-lined greens at this par-72, 6,455-yard course affords magnificent views of the Ko'olau and Wai'anae mountain ranges around it. *95-176 Kuahelani Ave., Mililani, tel. 808/623–2222, www.mililanigolf.com. Greens fee $89, cart included.*

Olomana Golf Links. This par-72, 6,326-yard course features hills and some interesting water hazards, not to mention a backdrop of the sheer cliffs of the Koʻolau Mountains. *41-1801 Kalanianaole Hwy., Waimānalo, tel. 808/259–7626. Greens fee $90, cart included.*

Mākaha Valley Country Golf Club. Two exceptional 18-hole courses here offer a beautiful valley setting. *84-626 Mākaha Valley Rd., Waiʻanae, tel. 808/695–9544 or 800/757–8060. Greens fee $125 until noon, $90 noon–2:30, $50 2:30–closing; cart included.*

Horseback Riding

Correa Trails Hawaii. Ride along trails that hug the Koʻolau Mountain range and offer ocean views of the spectacular Waimānalo coast. Rates are $50 for a one-hour ride and $75 for a two-hour trek. *41-050 Kalanianaole Hwy., Waimānalo, tel. 808/ 259–9005.*

Kualoa Ranch. This ranch across from Kualoa Beach Park leads trail rides in Kaʻaʻawa, one of the most beautiful valleys in all Hawaiʻi. Trail rides cost between $35 and $99. Kualoa has other activities as well, such as windsurfing, jet skiing, all-terrain-vehicle trail rides, and children's activities. *49-560 Kamehameha Hwy., Kaʻaʻawa, tel. 808/237–7321.*

Waimea Falls Park. Take a guided horseback trail ride through the verdant Waimea Valley. Admission is $24 to the park, with various additional charges depending on activity package option chosen. *59-864 Kamehameha Hwy., Haliewa, tel. 808/ 638–5300.*

Jogging

In Honolulu, the most popular places to jog are the two parks, **Kapiʻolani** and **Ala Moana,** at either end of Waikīkī. In both cases, the loop around the park is just under 2 mi. You can run a 4½-mi ring around **Diamond Head crater,** past scenic views, luxurious homes, and herds of other joggers. If you're looking for jogging companions, show up for the free **Honolulu Marathon Clinic,** which starts at the Kapiʻolani Bandstand from March through November, Sunday at 7:30 AM.

Once you leave Honolulu, it gets trickier to find places to jog that are scenic as well as safe. It's best to stick to the well-traveled routes, or ask the experienced folks at the **Running Room** (819 Kapahulu Ave., Kapahulu, Honolulu, tel. 808/737–2422) for advice.

The "Honolulu Walking Map" and "The Fitness Fun Map" are free from the **Hawaiʻi State Department of Health** (1250 Punchbowl St., Room 217, Downtown Honolulu, Honolulu, tel. 808/586–4661). These list more than two dozen routes and suggested itineraries for seeing Oʻahu on foot.

Tennis

Oʻahu has 181 public tennis courts that are free and open for play on a first-come, first-served basis; you're limited to 45 minutes of court time if others are waiting to play. A complete listing is available free of charge from the **Department of Parks and Recreation** (Tennis Unit, 650 S. King St., Honolulu 96813, tel. 808/971–7150, www.co.honolulu.hi.us).

Kapiʻolani Park, on the Diamond Head end of Waikīkī, has two tennis locations. The **Diamond Head Tennis Center** (3908 Pākī Ave., tel. 808/971–7150), on the mauka side of Kapiʻolani Park, has nine courts open to the public. There are more than a dozen courts for play at **Kapiʻolani Tennis Courts** (2748 Kalākaua Ave., tel. 808/971–2510). The closest public courts to the ewa end of Waikīkī are in **Ala Moana Park** (Makai side of Ala Moana Blvd., tel. 808/592–7031).

A few Waikīkī hotels have tennis courts that are open to nonguests for a fee. There's one championship tennis court located on the third-floor recreation deck of the **Waikīkī Beach Marriott Resort** (2552 Kalākaua Ave., tel. 808/922–6611). Two tennis courts and tennis lessons are available at the **Pacific Beach Hotel** (2490 Kalākaua Ave., Waikīkī, tel. 808/922–1233).

Forty-five minutes from Waikīkī, on O'ahu's Ewa Plain, are two championship tennis courts at the **Hawai'i Prince Golf Club** (91-1200 Ft. Weaver Rd., 'Ewa Beach, tel. 808/944–4567); shuttle service is available from the Hawai'i Prince Hotel Waikīkī for hotel guests.

Water Park

Hawaiian Waters Adventure Park. Get wet and wild at this 29-acre water-theme park with a football field–size wave pool, inner-tube cruising, and multistory waterslides. A children's water land of delight has a kiddie pool, waterfalls, minislides, and animal floaties. It's in Kapolei, mauka of the H-1 Freeway on Farrington Highway, 15 minutes from the Honolulu International Airport. *400 Farrington Hwy., Kapolei, tel. 808/674–9283, www.hawaiianwaters.com. $30. 10:30–5:30, longer hours in summer.*

Water Sports

The seemingly endless ocean options can be arranged through any hotel travel desk or beach concession. Try the **Waikīkī Beach Center,** next to the Sheraton Moana Surfrider, or the **C & K Beach Service,** by the Hilton Hawaiian Village (no telephones).

DEEP-SEA FISHING
Inter-Island Sportfishing (tel. 808/591–8888) operates four vessels available for exclusive or shared deep-sea fishing charters. Rates range from $165 to $1,000 per day, depending on whether you choose an exclusive charter or share one with five other anglers. If the "big one" doesn't get away, Inter-

Island will arrange to have your trophy fish mounted and sent to you. Departures for charters are from Kewalo Basin. **Magic Sportfishing** (tel. 808/596–2998) offers shared and private charters; rates range from $120 to $650 per day.

OCEAN KAYAKING

This dynamic sport is catching on fast in the Islands. On the North Shore, kayak lessons are available from **Kayak Oʻahu Adventures** (Waimea Valley Adventures Park, 59-894 Kamehameha Hwy., tel. 808/638–8189). You can kayak the "surfing waters of the kings" off Waikīkī with assistance from **Prime Time Sports** (Ft. DeRussy Beach, tel. 808/949–8952). Bob Twogood, a name that is synonymous with Oʻahu kayaking, runs a shop called **Twogood Kayaks Hawaiʻi** (345 Hahani St., Kailua, tel. 808/262–5656, www.aloha.com/~twogood), which makes, rents, and sells the fiberglass craft. Twogood rents solo kayaks for $25 a half day, and $32 for a full day. Tandems are $32 a half day and $42 for a full day, including kayak delivery and pickup across from Kailua Beach.

SAILING

Honolulu Sailing Company (tel. 808/239–3900, www.honsail.com) offers a variety of sailing options as well as sailing instruction. Departures are from Pier 2, Honolulu Harbor.

SCUBA DIVING AND SNORKELING

South Seas Aquatics (tel. 808/922–0852) offers two-tank boat dives at various sites for $75. Several certification courses are available; call for rates. On the North Shore, **Surf-N-Sea** (tel. 808/637–9887) conducts a variety of dive excursions, including night dives. A two-tank excursion starts at $65. Night dives begin at $80.

The most famous snorkeling spot in Hawaiʻi is Hanauma Bay. You can get masks, fins, and snorkels at the **rental stand** (tel. 808/395–4725) right at the park. **Hanauma Bay Snorkeling Excursions** (tel. 808/373–5060) provides transport from Waikīkī and costs $20 round-trip, including park admission, snorkeling gear, and lessons. You can pick up snorkeling equipment and site advice from **Snorkel Bob's** (700 Kapahulu Ave., tel. 808/735-7944), conveniently located on the way to Hanauma Bay.

Area dive sites include the following:

Hanauma Bay. East of Koko Head, this bay is an underwater state park and a popular dive site. The shallow inner reef gradually drops from 10 ft to 70 ft at the outer reef. Expect to see butterfly fish, goatfish, parrot fish, surgeon fish, and sea turtles.

Mahi Wai'anae. This 165-ft minesweeper was sunk in 1982 in the waters just south of Wai'anae on O'ahu's leeward coast to create an artificial reef. It's intact and penetrable. Goatfish, tame lemon butterfly fish, blue-striped snapper, and 6-ft moray eels can be seen hanging out here. Depths are from 50 ft to 90 ft.

Maunalua Bay. East of Diamond Head, Maunalua Bay has several sites, including Turtle Canyon, with lava flow ridges and sandy canyons teeming with green sea turtles of all sizes; *Kāhala Barge*, a penetrable, 200-ft sunken vessel; Big Eel Reef, with many varieties of moray eels; and Fantasy Reef, a series of lava ledges and archways populated with barracuda and eels.

Shark's Cove. This North Shore site is diveable in the summer months only and should be explored only by experienced divers. Sunlight from above creates a stained-glass effect in the large, roomy caverns. Easily accessible from shore, the cove's depths range from 15 ft to 45 ft. This is the most popular cavern dive on the island.

Three Tables. Named for the trio of flat rocks that break the surface near the beach, this North Shore site has easy access from the shore. Beneath the waves are large rock formations, caverns, and ledges. It's diveable only in the summer months.

SURFING

To rent a board in Waikīkī, visit **C&K Beach Service** (no phone), on the beach fronting the Hilton Hawaiian Village. Rentals cost $8 to $10 per hour, depending on the size of the board, and $12 for two hours. Small group lessons are $30 per hour with board, and they promise to have you riding the waves by lesson's end.

Novice surfers can meet with guaranteed success with lessons from the **Palakaiko Beach Boys Club** (no phone), who have lessons available every half hour on famous Kūhiō Beach.

Surfing and bodysurfing instruction from the staff of Hans Hedemann, who spent 17 years himself on the professional surfer World Tour circuit, is available for $50 per hour for group lessons and $90 for private lessons at the Waikīkī **Hans Hedemann Surfing School** (tel. 808/924–7778).

On the North Shore, rent a short board for $5 an hour or a long board for $7 from a shop called **Surf 'N' Sea** (tel. 808/637–9887). Its surfing lessons cost $65 for three hours and start daily at 1 PM. Or contact **North Shore Eco-Surf Tours** (808/638–9503) for a surf tour that is not only exhilarating but educational, too.

WATERSKIING

Hawaii Sports Wakeboard and Water Ski Center (Koko Marina Shopping Center, 7192 Kalaniana'ole Hwy., Hawai'i Kai, tel. 808/395–3773) has a package with round-trip transportation from Waikīkī and a half day of waterskiing in Hawai'i Kai Marina for $110 per hour per person (two-person minimum), with lessons. There are also rides in inflatable banana boats and bumper tubes for children of all ages.

WINDSURFING

This sport was born in Hawai'i, and O'ahu's Kailua Beach is its cradle. **Kailua Sailboard and Kayaks Company** (130 Kailua Rd., Kailua, tel. 808/262–2555) offers small group lessons, rents equipment, and transports everything to the waterfront. World champion Robby Naish and his family build and sell boards, rent equipment, provide accommodations referrals, and offer windsurfing and kiteboarding instruction out of **Naish Hawai'i** (155A Hamakua Dr., Kailua, tel. 808/261–6067, www.naish.com). A four-hour package, including 90 minutes of instruction, costs $55. **Surf 'N' Sea** (7192 Kalaniana'ole Hwy., Hale'iwa, tel. 808/637–9887) rents windsurfing gear for $12 per hour; a two-hour windsurfing lesson costs $58.**Windsurfing School North Shore** (59-452 Makana Rd., Hale'iwa, tel. 808/638–8198) offers expert instruction, but you have to bring your own board.

SPECTATOR SPORTS

Football

The nationally televised **NFL Pro Bowl** (tel. 808/486–9300) is held in early February at Aloha Stadium in Honolulu. For local action the **University of Hawai'i Warriors** (tel. 808/956–6508) take to the field at Aloha Stadium in season, with a big local following. There are often express buses to games from Kapi'olani Park.

Golf

The giants of the greens return to Hawai'i every January or February (depending on the TV scheduling) to compete in the **Sony Open Golf Tournament** (tel. 808/734–2151), a PGA tour regular with a $1 million purse. It's held at the exclusive Wai'alae Country Club in Kāhala, and it's always a crowd pleaser.

Running

The **Honolulu Marathon** is a thrilling event to watch as well as to participate in. Join the throngs who cheer at the finish line at Kapi'olani Park as internationally famous and local runners tackle the 26.2-mi challenge. It's held on the second Sunday in

Smart Sightseeings

Savvy travelers and others who take their sightseeing seriously have skills worth knowing about.

DON'T PLAN YOUR VISIT IN YOUR HOTEL ROOM Don't wait until you pull into town to decide how to spend your days. It's inevitable that there will be much more to see and do than you'll have time for: choose sights in advance.

ORGANIZE YOUR TOURING Note the places that most interest you on a map, and visit places that are near each other during the same morning or afternoon.

START THE DAY WELL EQUIPPED Leave your hotel in the morning with everything you need for the day—maps, medicines, extra film, your guidebook, rain gear, and another layer of clothing in case the weather turns cooler.

TOUR MUSEUMS EARLY If you're there when the doors open you'll have an intimate experience of the collection.

EASY DOES IT See museums in the mornings, when you're fresh, and visit sit-down attractions later on. Take breaks before you need them.

STRIKE UP A CONVERSATION Only curmudgeons don't respond to a smile and a polite request for information. Most people appreciate your interest in their home town. And your conversations may end up being your most vivid memories.

GET LOST When you do, you never know what you'll find—but you can count on it being memorable. Use your guidebook to help you get back on track. Build wandering-around time into every day.

QUIT BEFORE YOU'RE TIRED There's no point in seeing that one extra sight if you're too exhausted to enjoy it.

TAKE YOUR MOTHER'S ADVICE Go to the bathroom when you have the chance. You never know what lies ahead.

December and is sponsored by the Honolulu Marathon Association (tel. 808/734–7200, www.honolulumarathon.org).

Surfing

In winter head out to the North Shore to watch the best surfers in the world hang ten during the **Van's Triple Crown Hawaiian Pro Surfing Championships** (tel. 808/596–7877). This two-day event, scheduled according to wave conditions, is generally held at the Banzai Pipeline and Sunset Beach during November and December.

Triathlon

Swim-bike-run events are gaining in popularity and number in Hawai'i. Most fun to watch (or compete in) is the **Tinman Triathlon** (tel. 808/732–7311), held in mid-July in Waikīkī.

Volleyball

Volleyball is extremely popular on the Islands, and no wonder. Both the men's and women's teams of the **University of Hawai'i** have blasted to a number-one ranking in years past. Crowded, noisy, and very exciting home games are played from September through December (women's) and from January through April (men's) in the university's 10,000-seat Stan Sheriff Arena. *Lower Campus Rd., Honolulu, tel. 808/956–4481. $8.*

Windsurfing

Watch the pros jump and spin on the waves during July's **Pan Am Hawaiian Windsurfing World Cup** (tel. 808/734–6999) off Kailua Beach. For windsurfing competitions off Diamond Head point, check out August's **Wahine Classic** (808/521–4322), featuring the world's best female boardsailors.

In This Chapter

Updated by Maggie Wunsch

nightlife and the arts

NIGHTLIFE ON O'AHU CAN BE AS SIMPLE as a barefoot stroll in the sand or as elaborate as a dinner show with all the glitter of a Las Vegas production. You can view the vibrant hues of a Honolulu sunset during a cocktail cruise or hear the melodies of ancient chants at a lū'au on a remote west-shore beach.

Waikīkī's Kalākaua and Kūhiō avenues come to life when the sun goes down. Outside Honolulu, offerings are slimmer but equally diverse. Check the local newspapers—the *Honolulu Advertiser*, the *Honolulu Star-Bulletin*, or the *Honolulu Weekly*—for the latest events.

BARS, CABARETS, AND CLUBS

Honolulu

AARON'S ATOP THE ALA MOANA. A splendid view, good contemporary dance music, and a sophisticated, well-dressed crowd come together at this Honolulu nightclub, which also offers a late-night dining menu. *Ala Moana Hotel, 410 Atkinson Dr., Ala Moana, tel. 808/955–4466. Dancing Sun.–Thurs. 9:30–2, Fri.–Sat. 10–2.*

ANNA BANNANA'S. Generations of Hawai'i college students have spent more than an evening or two at this legendary two-story, smoky dive. Here, the music is fresh, loud, and sometimes experimental. Local favorites deliver ultracreative dance music, and the likes of blues singer Taj Mahal have been known to perform. 2440 S. Beretania St., Mōʻiliʻili, tel. 808/946–5190. Nightly 11:30–2, live music Thurs.–Sat. 9–2.

BANYAN COURTYARD. The Banyan Courtyard is steeped in history. From this location the radio program *Hawaiʻi Calls* first broadcast the sounds of Hawaiian music and the rolling surf to a U.S. mainland audience in 1935. Today, a variety of Hawaiian entertainment continues to provide the perfect accompaniment to the sounds of the surf just steps away. *Sheraton Moana Surfrider, 2365 Kalākaua Ave., Waikīkī, tel. 808/922–3111. Nightly 5:30–11.*

CHAI'S ISLAND BISTRO. Chai's welcomes some of Hawaiʻi's top entertainers, such as the Brothers Cazimero, Hapa, and the Makaha Sons. There's also a Pacific Rim–cuisine menu with a twist of Thai. *Aloha Tower Marketplace, 1 Aloha Tower Dr., Downtown Honolulu, tel. 808/585–0011. Nightly from 4; music performances nightly at 7.*

ESPRIT. Popular Honolulu bands performing Top 40 hits are regulars here. This club, in the heart of Waikīkī, is a popular dance spot for all ages. *Sheraton Waikīkī, 2255 Kalākaua Ave., Waikīkī, tel. 808/922–4422. Sat.–Mon. 8:30 PM–1 AM.*

GORDON BIERSCH BREWERY RESTAURANT. Live duos and trios serenade patrons of the outside bar that flanks Honolulu Harbor. Although there's no dancing, this is the place in Honolulu to see and be seen. *Aloha Tower Marketplace, 1 Aloha Tower Dr., Downtown Honolulu, tel. 808/599–4877. Wed.–Sat. 7–1.*

HANOHANO ROOM. World-class views 30 stories above Waikīkī, and the soft sounds of "Stardust" make this a romantic spot for those who like to dance close and slow. *Sheraton Waikīkī, 2255 Kalākaua Ave., 30th floor, Waikīkī, tel. 808/922–4422. Sat. 11–1.*

HONU BAR AND TERRACE. Sophisticated and swank, this lobby lounge presents light jazz and island ensembles during the cocktail and sunset hours. *Kāhala Mandarin Oriental Hawai'i, 5000 Kāhala Ave., Kāhala, tel. 808/739–8888. Mon.–Thurs. 4:30–6:30, Fri.–Sun. 5–7.*

HULA'S BAR AND LEI STAND. Hawai'i's oldest and best known gay-friendly nightspot offers calming panoramic outdoor views of Diamond Head and the Pacific Ocean from the bar by day and a high-energy club scene by night. *Waikīkī Grand Hotel, 134 Kapahulu Ave., 2nd floor, Waikīkī, tel. 808/923–0669. Daily, 10 AM–2 AM, $3 cover after 10 PM.*

MAI TAI BAR. Keith and Carmen Haugen sing island duets at this open-air Waikīkī Beach bar. Carmen's hula is a thing of beauty. Catch them in the early evenings Tuesday and Wednesday. Entertainers vary on other nights. *Royal Hawaiian Hotel, 2259 Kalākaua Ave., Waikīkī, tel. 808/923–0669. Entertainment nightly 5:30–7:30.*

MOOSE McGILLYCUDDY'S PUB AND CAFE. Loud bands play for the beach-and-beer gang in a blue-jeans-and-T-shirt setting. *310 Lewers St., Waikīkī, tel. 808/923–0751. Nightly 9–1:30.*

NASHVILLE WAIKĪKĪ. Country music in the tropics? You bet! Put on your *paniolo* (Hawaiian cowboy) duds and mosey on out to the giant dance floor. There are pool tables, dartboards, line dancing, and free dance lessons to boot. *Ohana Waikīkī West Hotel, 2330 Kūhiō Ave., Waikīkī, tel. 808/926–7911. Daily 4–4; dance lessons nightly at 7.*

PARADISE LOUNGE. Several contemporary Hawaiian acts, including the longtime band Olomana, perform in this pretty outdoor club. *Hilton Hawaiian Village, 2005 Kālia Rd., Waikīkī, tel. 808/949–4321. Fri.–Sat. 8–midnight.*

PIER BAR. Here's one of the few places in Honolulu where you can hear live music outdoors and dance underneath the stars. It attracts a grab bag of groups; call ahead to find out who's playing. *Aloha Tower Marketplace, 1 Aloha Tower Dr., Downtown Honolulu, tel. 808/536–2166. Nightly 6:30–4.*

PIPELINE CAFE AND SPORTS BAR. This is two stories of fun with pool, darts, and more. The upstairs sports bar is for watching sports on TV; dancing takes place downstairs to both live musical acts and DJs. *805 Pohukaina St., Kaka'ako, tel. 808/589–1999. Nightly 8–4.*

ROYAL GARDEN AT WAIKĪKĪ. Some of O'ahu's top jazz stylists perform in the elegant, intimate lobby lounge of this sophisticated hotel. *Royal Garden at Waikīkī, 444 'Olohana St., Waikīkī, tel. 808/943–0202. Tues.–Sun. 8–11.*

RUMOURS. The after-work crowd loves this spot, which has dance videos, disco, and throbbing lights. On Saturday "Little Chill" nights, the club plays oldies from the '70s and '80s and serves free pūpū. There is "salsa after dark" dancing Thursday evening. *Ala Moana Hotel, 410 Atkinson St., Ala Moana, tel. 808/955–4811. Wed.–Fri. 5–2, Sat. 8–4.*

SHORE BIRD BEACH BROILER. This Waikīkī beachfront disco spills right out onto the sand. It has a large dance floor and a 10-ft video screen. Karaoke sing-alongs are held nightly. *Outrigger Reef Hotel on the Beach, 2169 Kālia Rd., Waikīkī, tel. 808/922–2887. Nightly 9–2.*

VENUS NIGHTCLUB. This high-energy social bar features hip-hop, trance, and reggae with guest DJs five nights a week. Attention, ladies: the male dance revue Saturday evening is a Honolulu experience. *1349 Kapi'olani Blvd., Ala Moana, tel. 808/955–2640. Nightly 8–4.*

VIRTUAL EXPERIENCE. Calling itself a place to escape, this posh, high-tech club has 12 oversize screens for exploring computerized worlds, an atmosphere conducive to quiet conversation, and drinks and pūpū to heighten the experience. *311 Lewers St.,*

Waikīkī, tel. 808/847–8825. Nightly 6–4. Live entertainment Tues. and Thurs.

WAVE WAIKĪKĪ. Dance to live rock and roll until 1:30 and recorded music after that. It can be a rough scene (it's seen more than its fair share of drunken fisticuffs), but the bands are tops. Late nights, the music here goes definitely "underground." *1877 Kalākaua Ave., Waikīkī, tel. 808/941–0424. Nightly 9–4.*

WORLD CAFE. Honolulu's only upscale billiards nightclub also has a sports bar and dancing to Top 40 tunes. *500 Ala Moana Blvd., Ala Moana, tel. 808/599–4450. Mon.–Thurs. 11:30 PM–2 AM, Fri.–Sat. 11:30 PM–4 AM, Sun. 3 PM–2 AM.*

ZANZABAR. DJs spin top hits, from hip-hop to soul, at this elegant and high-energy nightspot in the Waikīkī Trade Center. *2255 Kūhiō Ave., Waikīkī, tel. 808/924–3939. Nightly 9–4.*

COCKTAIL AND DINNER CRUISES

Dinner cruises depart either from the piers adjacent to the Aloha Tower Marketplace in downtown Honolulu or from Kewalo Basin, just 'ewa of Ala Moana Beach Park, and head along the coast toward Diamond Head. There's usually dinner, dancing, drinks, and a sensational sunset. Except as noted, dinner cruises cost approximately $50–$60, cocktail cruises $20–$30. Most major credit cards are accepted.

ALI'I KAI CATAMARAN. Patterned after an ancient Polynesian vessel, this huge catamaran casts off from Aloha Tower with 1,000 passengers. The deluxe dinner cruise has two open bars, a huge dinner, and an authentic Polynesian show with colorful hula music. The food is good, the after-dinner show loud and fun, and everyone dances on the way back to shore. *Pier 5, street level, Honolulu, tel. 808/539–9400.*

DREAM CRUISES. The 100-ft motor yacht *American Dream* handles up to 225 guests for evening cruises off the shores of

Waikīkī. Decks have plenty of outdoor space for views of the twinkling city lights. The dinner cruise includes one mai tai, buffet, and soft drinks. You pay for extra drinks. After a hula demonstration with audience participation, a disc jockey spins dancing tunes from the '50s through the '70s. 306 Kamani St., Honolulu, tel. 808/592–5200 or 800/400–7300, www.dream-cruises.com.

NAVATEK CRUISES. The sleek Navatek is a revolutionary craft designed to sail smoothly in rough waters, which allows it to power farther along Waikīkī's coastline than its competitors. Choose from sunset dinner or moonlight cruises, or breakfast and lunch whale-watch cruises December through mid-April. Tours leave from Pier 6, next to Aloha Tower Marketplace. Honolulu Harbor, tel. 808/973–1311, goatlantis.com.

PARADISE CRUISES. Prices vary depending on which deck you choose on the 1,600-passenger, four-deck Star of Honolulu. For instance, a seven-course French-style dinner and live jazz on the top deck costs $199. A steak and crab feast on level two costs $72. Evening excursions also take place on the 340-passenger Starlet I and 230-passenger Starlet II. 1540 S. King St., Honolulu, tel. 808/983–7827, www.paradisecruises.com.

COCKTAIL AND DINNER SHOWS

Some Oʻahu entertainers have been around for years, and others have just arrived on the scene. Either way, the dinner-show food is usually buffet-style with a definite local accent. Dinner shows are all in the $45 to $60 range. Cocktail shows run $30 to $35. The prices usually include one cocktail, tax, and gratuity. In all cases, reservations are essential, and most major credit cards are accepted. Be sure to call in advance. You never know when an artist may have switched venues.

ALOHA LAS VEGAS REVUE. A Las Vegas–style revue featuring impersonators in the style of top performers of pop, rock, and country music. Waikīkī Beachcomber Hotel, 2300 Kalākaua Ave.,

Waikīkī, tel. 808/971–4345 or 877/971–7414. Shows Tues., Thurs., and Sat. at 9:40.

CREATION: A POLYNESIAN ODYSSEY. This show traces Hawai'i's culture and history, from its origins to statehood. The highlight is a daring Samoan fire knife dancer. *'Āinahau Showroom, Sheraton Princess Ka'iulani Hotel, 120 Ka'iulani Ave., Waikīkī, tel. 808/931–4660. Dinner shows Tues.,Thurs., and Sat. at 6:30.*

DON HO. Don Ho is the singer who put Waikīkī entertainment on the map. His song "Tiny Bubbles" would become his trademark. His show, a Polynesian revue (with a cast of young and attractive Hawaiian performers), has found the perfect home in this intimate club inside the Waikīkī Beachcomber Hotel. *Waikīkī Beachcomber Hotel, 2300 Kalākaua Ave., Waikīkī, tel. 808/923–3981. Shows Sun.–Thurs. at 7, with cocktail and dinner seatings.*

MAGIC OF POLYNESIA. Hawai'i's top illusionist, John Hirokawa, displays mystifying sleight of hand in this highly entertaining show that incorporates contemporary hula and island music into its acts. *Waikīkī Beachcomber Hotel, 2300 Kalākaua Ave., Waikīkī, tel. 808/971–4321. Nightly at 6:30 and 8:45.*

POLYNESIAN CULTURAL CENTER. Easily one of the best on the Islands, this show has soaring moments and an "erupting volcano." The performers are students from Brigham Young University's Hawai'i campus. *55-370 Kamehameha Hwy., Lā'ie, tel. 808/293–3333, www.polynesia.com. Dinner seating Mon.–Sat. at 4:30; show Apr.–May and Sept.–Dec. 25, Mon.–Sat. at 7:30, and Dec. 26–Mar. and June–Aug., Mon.–Sat. at 6 and 7:45.*

SOCIETY OF SEVEN. This lively, popular septet has great staying power and, after more than 25 years, continues to put on one of the best shows in Waikīkī. They sing; dance; do impersonations; play instruments; and, above all, entertain with their contemporary sound. *Outrigger Waikīkī on the Beach, 2335 Kalākaua Ave., Waikīkī, tel. 808/923–7469. Mon.–Sat. at 8:30.*

DANCE

Every year at least one of mainland America's finer ballet troupes makes the trip to Honolulu for a series of dance performances at the **Neal Blaisdell Center Concert Hall** (Ward Ave. at King St., Honolulu, tel. 808/591–2211). A local company, **Ballet Hawai'i** (tel. 808/988–7578), is active during the holiday season with its annual production of *The Nutcracker*, which is usually held at the Mamiya Theater (St. Louis School, 3142 Wai'alae Ave., Kaimukī, Honolulu).

FILM

Art, international, classic, and silent films are screened at the little theater at the **Honolulu Academy of Arts** (900 S. Beretania St., Downtown Honolulu, Honolulu, tel. 808/532–8768). **Kāhala Mall** (4211 Wai'alae Ave., Kāhala, Honolulu, tel. 808/733–6233) has eight movie theaters showing a diverse range of films. It's a 10-minute drive from Waikīkī. **Varsity Twins Theater** (1106 University Ave., Mō'ili'ili, Honolulu, tel. 808/973–5834) is the site for showings of internationally acclaimed independent art films. **Waikīkī 's Theatres 1, 2, and 3** (333 Seaside Avenue (1 and 2), Kalākaua at Seaside (3), tel. 808/971–5032), located in the heart of Waikīkī, offer first-run films with numerous showings throughout the day. The **Hawai'i International Film Festival** (tel. 808/528–3456) may not be Cannes, but it is unique and exciting. During the weeklong festival, held from the end of November to early December, top films from the United States, Asia, and the Pacific are screened day and night at several theaters on O'ahu.

LŪ'AU

GERMAINE'S LŪ'AU. This lū'au is billed as being "100 years away from Waikīkī." Expect a lively crowd as you are bused to a private beach 35 minutes from Waikīkī. The bus ride is actually a lot of fun, and the beach and the sunset are pleasant. The service is brisk in order to feed everyone on time, and the food is the usual multicourse, all-you-can-eat buffet, but the show is warm and friendly. tel. 808/949–6626 or 800/367–5665. Tues.–Sat. at 6.

PARADISE COVE LŪ'AU. There are palms and a glorious sunset, and the pageantry is fun, even informative. The food—well, you didn't come for the food, did you? This is another mass-produced event for 1,000 or so. A bus takes you from one of six Waikīkī hotel pickup points to a remote beachfront estate beside a picturesque cove on the western side of the island, 27 mi from Waikīkī. tel. 808/842–5911, www.paradisecovehawaii.com. Daily at 5:30, doors open at 5.

POLYNESIAN CULTURAL CENTER ALI'I LŪ'AU. An hour's drive from Honolulu, this North Shore O'ahu lū'au is set amid seven re-created villages of Polynesia. Dinner is all-you-can-eat traditional lū'au food such as kalua pig and lomi lomi salmon, followed by a world-class revue. tel. 808/293–3333 or 800/367–7060, www.polynesia.com. Mon.–Sat. at 5:30.

ROYAL HAWAIIAN LŪ'AU. Waikīkī's only oceanfront lū'au offers an exotic, upscale menu and entertainment. With the setting sun, Diamond Head, the Pacific Ocean, and the legendary Pink Palace as backdrop, this contemporary lū'au might even make you learn to love poi. tel. 808/923–7311. Mon. and Thurs. at 6.

MUSIC

CHAMBER MUSIC HAWAI'I (tel. 808/947–1975) gives 25 concerts a year at the **Honolulu Lutheran Church** (1730 Punahou St., Makiki Heights, Honolulu), **Honolulu Academy of Arts** (900 S. Beretania St., Downtown Honolulu, Honolulu), and other locations around the island.

HAWAI'I OPERA THEATER's season spans January through March and includes such works as *The Barber of Seville, Tristan and Isolde,* and *Madame Butterfly*. All are performed in their original language with projected English translation at the **Neal Blaisdell Concert Hall** (Neal Blaisdell Concert Hall, Ward Ave.

and King St., Downtown Honolulu, Honolulu, tel. 808/596–7858. $25–$79 at box office).

The **Honolulu Symphony Orchestra** (677 Ala Moana Blvd., Downtown Honolulu, Honolulu, tel. 808/792–2000, www.honolulusymphony.com. $10–$50) performs at the Neil Blaisdell Concert Hall and is led by the young, dynamic Samuel Wong. The Honolulu Pops series, with some performances underneath the stars summer nights at the Waikīkī Shell, features top local and national artists under the direction of talented conductor-composer Matt Catingub.

Rock concerts are usually performed at the domed **Neal Blaisdell Center Arena** (tel. 808/591–2211). Internationally famous performers pack them in at **Aloha Stadium** (tel. 808/486–9300).

THEATER

Because many of today's touring shows and music artists depend on major theatrical sets, lighting, and sound, Hawai'i, already pricey, can be an expensive gig. As a result, major touring companies who do manage to stop here sell out fast.

ARMY COMMUNITY THEATRE. This is a favorite for its revivals of musical theater classics, presented in an 800-seat house. The casts are talented, and the fare is great for families. *Richardson Theater, Fort Shafter, Downtown Honolulu, Honolulu, tel. 808/438–4480. $12–$15.*

DIAMOND HEAD THEATER. The repertoire includes a little of everything: musicals, dramas, experimental productions, and classics. This company is in residence five minutes from Waikīkī, right next to Diamond Head. *520 Makapu'u Ave., Kapahulu, Honolulu, tel. 808/734–0274. $10–$40.*

HAWAI'I THEATRE CENTER. Beautifully restored, this downtown Honolulu theater built in the 1920s in a neoclassic beaux-arts style hosts a wide range of unique events, including international theatrical productions. Historic tours of the theater are offered Tuesday at 11 for $5. *1130 Bethel St., Downtown Honolulu, Honolulu, tel. 808/528–0506, www.hawaiitheatre.com. Prices vary.*

🐣 **HONOLULU THEATER FOR YOUTH.** This group stages delightful productions for children around the Islands from September through May. Call for a schedule. *2846 Ualena St., Downtown Honolulu, Honolulu, tel. 808/839–9885. $10.*

JOHN F. KENNEDY THEATER. Eclectic dramatic offerings—everything from musical theater to Kabuki, Nō, and Chinese opera—are performed at this space at the University of Hawai'i's Mānoa campus. *1770 East–West Rd., Mānoa, Honolulu, tel. 808/956–7655. $9–$12.*

KUMU KAHUA. This is the only troupe presenting shows and plays written by local playwrights about the Islands. It stages five or six productions a year. *46 Merchant St., Downtown Honolulu, Honolulu, tel. 808/536–4441. $12–$15.*

MĀNOA VALLEY THEATER. Wonderful nonprofessional performances are put on in this intimate theater in Mānoa Valley from September through July. *2833 E. Mānoa Rd., Mānoa, Honolulu, tel. 808/988–6131. $17–$20.*

In This Chapter

Updated by Maggie Wunsch

where to stay

IF YOUR DREAM VACATION entails getting away from the usual hustle and bustle, look at the listings in the Around the Island category. If you prefer to be close to the action, go for a hotel or condominium in or near Waikīkī, where most of the island's lodgings are. Except for the peak months of January and February, you'll have little trouble getting a room if you call in advance. Don't be intimidated by published rates. Most hotels offer a variety of package options and special deals, such as sports, honeymoon, room and car, and kids stay/eat free promotions. These extras can make vacations even more affordable, so ask about them when you book.

Below is a selective list of lodging choices in each price category. For a complete list of every hotel and condominium on the island, write or call the Hawai'i Visitors & Convention Bureau for a free *Accommodation Guide*.

CATEGORY	COST*
$$$$	over $200
$$$	$125–$200
$$	$75–$125
$	under $75

All prices are for a standard double room, excluding 11.25% tax and service charges.

WAIKĪKĪ

$$$$ ASTON WAIKĪKĪ BEACH TOWER. On Kalākaua Avenue, but set back from the street on the mauka side, this 39-story luxury condominium resort has the atmosphere of an intimate vest-pocket hotel. The property has the usual amenities, oversize rooms, and views of Waikīkī that you'd expect from a larger beachfront resort. Stylish one- and two-bedroom suites have complete kitchens, washer-dryers, and private lānai. *2470 Kalākaua Ave., Waikīkī, Honolulu 96815, tel. 808/926–6400 or 800/922–7866, fax 808/926–7380, www.aston-hotels.com. 140 suites. Kitchenettes, minibars, pool, sauna, concierge. AE, D, DC, MC, V.*

\$\$\$\$ HALEKŪLANI. The sleek, modern, and luxurious oceanside
★ Halekūlani exemplifies the translation of its name—the "house befitting heaven." The service is impeccable, and the mood is tranquil amid the frenetic activity of Waikīkī. Guest rooms are spacious, and artfully appointed in marble and wood; most have ocean views, and each has its own lānai. *2199 Kālia Rd., Waikīkī, Honolulu 96815, tel. 808/923–2311 or 800/367–2343, fax 808/926–8004, www.halekulani.com. 412 rooms, 44 suites. 3 restaurants, room service, in-room data ports, in-room safes, minibars, pool, gym, hair salon, massage, beach, 3 bars, shops, dry cleaning, concierge, business services, meeting room. AE, DC, MC, V.*

\$\$\$\$ HAWAIʻI PRINCE HOTEL WAIKĪKĪ. The Prince is a slim high-rise with the kind of sophisticated interior design generally reserved for a city hotel. You know you're in Waikīkī, however, when you look out your window at the Ala Wai Yacht Harbor. Guest rooms have floor-to-ceiling windows with ocean views. This hotel also has its own 27-hole Arnold Palmer–designed golf course in Ewa Beach, about a 45-minute hotel shuttle ride from Waikīki. *100 Holomoana St., Waikīkī, Honolulu 96815, tel. 808/956–1111 or 800/321–6248, fax 808/946–0811, www.hawaiiprincehotel.com. 467 rooms, 54 suites. 3 restaurants, room service, in-room data ports, in-room safes, minibars, 27-hole golf course, pool, gym, hair salon, hot tub, shops, baby-sitting, concierge, business services, meeting room. AE, DC, MC, V.*

\$\$\$\$ HILTON HAWAIIAN VILLAGE BEACH RESORT AND SPA. Sprawling
★ over 20 acres on Waikīkī's widest stretch of beach, this resort is

made up of five hotel towers surrounded by lavish gardens, cascading waterfalls, and 60 species of exotic birds, fish, and fauna. Choose from standard hotel guest rooms to one- or two-bedroom condo-style accommodations. Check out the sublime Mandara Spa and Holistic Wellness Center. *2005 Kālia Rd., Waikīkī, Honolulu 96815, tel. 808/949–4321 or 800/445–8667, fax 808/947–7898, www.hawaiianvillage.hilton.com. 2,180 rooms, 365 suites. 6 restaurants, room service, in-room data ports, in-room safes, minibars, 3 pools, gym, spa, beach, snorkeling, 4 bars, shops, children's programs (ages 5–12), dry cleaning, laundry service, concierge, business services, meeting room, car rental. AE, D, DC, MC, V.*

$$$$ HYATT REGENCY WAIKĪKĪ RESORT AND SPA. An open-air atrium with a two-story waterfall, shops, live music, and Harry's Bar make this one of the liveliest lobbies anywhere, though you may get lost in it. Guest rooms have private lānai and are decorated in soft creams and ocean blues. The Na Hoʻola Spa will pamper you with a poolside massage. The hotel is across from Kūhiō Beach and a short walk from Kapiʻolani Park. *2424 Kalākaua Ave., Waikīkī, Honolulu 96815, tel. 808/923–1234 or 800/233–1234, fax 808/923–7839, www.hyattwaikiki.com. 1,212 rooms, 18 suites. 4 restaurants, room service, in-room data ports, in-room safes, pool, spa, bar, lobby lounge, shops, children's programs (ages 5–12), concierge, business services. AE, D, DC, MC, V.*

$$$$ OUTRIGGER WAIKĪKĪ ON THE BEACH. Outrigger Hotels & Resorts' star property on Kalākaua Avenue stands oceanfront to some of the nicest sands in Waikīkī. Rooms have a Polynesian motif, and each has a lānai. For more than 25 years, the main ballroom has been home to the sizzling Society of Seven entertainers. The beachfront Duke's Canoe Club is a dining hot spot. *2335 Kalākaua Ave., Waikīkī, Honolulu 96815, tel. 808/923–0711 or 800/688–7444, fax 800/622–4852, www.outrigger.com. 500 rooms, 30 suites. 6 restaurants, room service, in-room data ports, in-room safes, minibars, pool, gym, hot tub, 5 bars, lobby lounge, shops, children's programs (ages*

waikīkī lodging

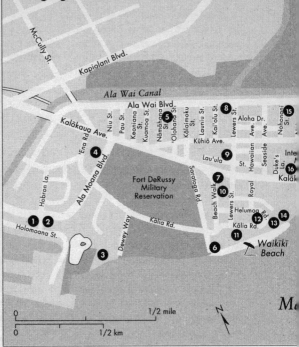

0 — 1/2 mile

0 — 1/2 km

N

Me

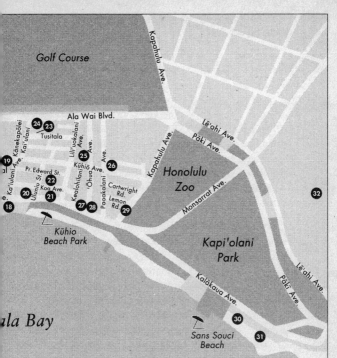

5–13), dry cleaning, laundry facilities, concierge, business services, meeting rooms. AE, D, DC, MC, V.

$$$$ RENAISSANCE 'ILIKAI WAIKĪKĪ. Spacious 600-square-ft guest rooms in two towers overlook Ala Wai Harbor and the ocean. The open-air lobby has cascading waterfalls; torches light the walkways for romantic evening strolls. Some guest rooms feature kitchenettes, and offer Internet access via television screens and cordless keyboards. 1777 Ala Moana Blvd., Waikīkī, Honolulu 96815, tel. 808/949–3811 or 800/645–5687, fax 808/947–0892, www.ilikaihotel.com. 728 rooms, 51 suites. 3 restaurants, room service, some kitchens, minibars, tennis court, 2 pools, health club, outdoor hot tub, massage, 2 lobby lounges, video game room, shops, laundry facilities, Internet, business services, meeting room, car rental. AE, D, DC, MC, V.

$$$$ ROYAL HAWAIIAN HOTEL. ★ Nicknamed the "Pink Palace of the Pacific" due to its architecture and pink exterior, the Royal was built in 1927 by Matson Navigation Company to accommodate its luxury-cruise passengers. The modern wing is more expensive, but for charm, the rooms in the Historic Wing, with their canopy beds and Queen Anne–style desks are a treasure. 2259 Kalākaua Ave., Waikīkī, Honolulu 96815, tel. 808/923–7311 or 800/782–9488, fax 808/924–7098, www.royal-hawaiian.com. 472 rooms, 53 suites. 3 restaurants, room service, minibars, pool, hair salon, spa, beach, bar, children's programs (ages 5–12), concierge, business services, meeting room. AE, DC, MC, V.

$$$$ SHERATON MOANA SURFRIDER. The Moana opened its doors in 1901, the first hotel on Waikīkī Beach. It has since merged with the newer Surfrider next door, but you can appreciate its history by requesting a room in the Moana Banyan Wing, where each floor is done in a different kind of wood—mahogany, maple, oak, cherry, and koa. These rooms are small by today's standards, but are well-appointed and charming. For accommodations with a modern feel, ask for the Diamond and Tower wings. 2365 Kalākaua Ave., Waikīkī, Honolulu 96815, tel. 808/922–3111 or 800/782–9488, fax 808/

923–0308, www.moana-surfrider.com. 750 rooms, 41 suites. 3 restaurants, snack bar, room service, minibars, pool, beach, bar, lobby lounge, concierge, meeting room. AE, DC, MC, V.

$$$$ SHERATON WAIKĪKĪ. Towering over its neighbors, the Sheraton takes center stage on Waikīkī Beach. Guest rooms are spacious, and many have grand views of Diamond Head. Be sure to take the glass-walled elevator up to the Hanohano Room, an elegant dining room with breathtaking panoramas of the ocean and Waikīkī. *2255 Kalākaua Ave., Waikīkī, Honolulu 96815, tel. 808/922–4422 or 800/325–3535, fax 808/923–8785, www.sheraton-hawaii.com. 1,709 rooms, 130 suites. 5 restaurants, minibars, room service, 2 pools, health club, beach, lobby lounge, dance club, shops, children's programs (ages 5–12), concierge, business services, meeting rooms. AE, DC, MC, V.*

$$$$ W HONOLULU—DIAMOND HEAD. The W is on the quiet edge of Waikīkī across from Kapiʻolani Park. Guest rooms feature private lānai, CD players, and VCRs with video library. The luxurious trademark W beds wrap you in 250-thread-count sheets, and rooms are elegantly appointed with teak furnishings, a Balinese island motif, and spectacular oceanfront views. The hotel's signature restaurant is the Diamond Head Grill. *2885 Kalākaua Ave., Waikīkī, Honolulu 96815, tel. 808/922–1700 or 888/528–9465, fax 808/923–2249. 44 rooms, 4 suites. Restaurant, room service, in-room data ports, in-room VCRs, beach, dry cleaning, laundry service, concierge, business services. AE, D, DC, MC, V.*

$$$$ WAIKĪKĪ BEACHCOMBER HOTEL. With an excellent location right
★ across the street from Waikīkī Beach, the Beachcomber is also a short walk from the Royal Hawaiian Shopping Center and the International Market Place. Rooms have contemporary furnishings, prints by local artists, and private lānai. Three evening shows are presented here: the venerable "Don Ho," "The Aloha Las Vegas Revue," and "The Magic of Polynesia." *2300 Kalākaua Ave., Waikīkī, Honolulu 96815, tel. 808/922–4646 or 800/622–4646, fax 808/923–4889, www.waikikibeachcomber.com. 487 rooms, 11 suites. Restaurant,*

lobby lounge, snack bar, minibars, no-smoking rooms, refrigerators, room service, pool. AE, DC, MC, V.

$$$–$$$$ ASTON WAIKĪKĪ SUNSET. Families enjoy this high-rise condominium resort near Diamond Head, one block from Waikīkī Beach and two blocks from the Honolulu Zoo. One- and two-bedroom suites have complete kitchens, daily maid service, and private lānai. There's also an outdoor barbecue area and a children's playground. *229 Paoakalani Ave., Waikīkī, Honolulu 96815, tel. 808/922–0511 or 800/922–7866, fax 808/922–8580, www.aston-hotels.com. 307 suites. Snack bar, kitchenettes, tennis court, pool, sauna, playground. AE, D, DC, MC, V.*

$$$–$$$$ DOUBLETREE ALANA WAIKĪKĪ. The lobby of this 19-story high-rise is modern and attractive, with rotating exhibits of local artists' work. Guest rooms have private lānai with panoramic views of Waikīkī, the ocean, or the mountains. Those doing business globally like the 24-hour business-center services. Also open round-the-clock is the fitness center. *1956 Ala Moana Blvd., Waikīkī, Honolulu 96815, tel. 808/941–7275 or 800/367–6070, fax 808/949–0996, www.alana-doubletree.com. 268 rooms, 45 suites. Restaurant, room service, minibars, pool, gym, lobby lounge, concierge, business services. AE, D, MC, V.*

$$$–$$$$ NEW OTANI KAIMANA BEACH HOTEL. Polished to a shine, this
★ hotel is open to the trade winds and furnished with big, comfortable chairs. The ambience is cheerful and charming, and the lobby has a happy, unpretentious feel. Best of all, it's right on the beach at the quiet end of Waikīkī, practically at the foot of Diamond Head. Rooms are smallish but very nicely appointed, with soothing pastel decor and off-white furnishings. *2863 Kalākaua Ave., Waikīkī, Honolulu 96815, tel. 808/923–1555 or 800/356–8264, fax 808/922–9404, www.kaimana.com. 119 rooms, 6 suites. 2 restaurants, room service, minibars, lobby lounge, meeting room. AE, D, DC, MC, V.*

$$$-$$$$ OUTRIGGER REEF ON THE BEACH. Right on the beach near Ft. DeRussy Park, the Reef is the official hotel for the Honolulu Marathon each December. Ask for an ocean view; the other rooms have decidedly less delightful overlooks. For fun, cook your own meal at the lively Shorebird Beach Broiler or pamper yourself at the oceanside Serenity Spa. *2169 Kālia Rd., Waikīkī, Honolulu 96815, tel. 808/923–3111 or 800/688–7444, fax 808/924–4957, www.outrigger.com. 846 rooms, 39 suites. 2 restaurants, room service, refrigerators, pool, gym, beach, 4 bars, nightclub, children's programs (ages 5–12), meeting room. AE, D, DC, MC, V.*

$$$-$$$$ RADISSON WAIKĪKĪ PRINCE KŪHIŌ. Two blocks from Kūhiō Beach, this 37-story high-rise is on the Diamond Head end of Waikīkī. Hawaiian-print bedspreads and artwork in sepia, cream, and earth tones decorate the rooms. *2500 Kūhiō Ave., Waikīkī, Honolulu 96815, tel. 808/922–8811 or 800/557–4422, fax 808/923–0330, www.radisson.com. 620 rooms. 2 restaurants, room service, in-room data ports, pool, gym, hot tub, lobby lounge, business services. AE, D, DC, MC, V.*

$$$-$$$$ WAIKĪKĪ BEACH MARRIOTT RESORT. On the eastern edge of Waikīkī, the hotel is across from Kūhiō Beach and close to Kapi'olani Park, the zoo, and the aquarium. Two towers have courtyards and public areas that are open to ocean breezes and sunlight. The Ali'iolani Tower's spacious guest rooms are some of the largest in Waikīkī, and the Paokalani Tower's Diamond Head side rooms offer breathtaking views of Diamond Head Crater and Kapi'olani Park. *2552 Kalākaua Ave., Waikīkī, Honolulu 96815, tel. 808/922–6611 or 800/367–5370, fax 808/921–5222, www. marriott.com. 1,337 rooms, 9 suites. 5 restaurants, lobby lounges, minibars, room service, 2 pools, tennis court, gym, dance club, concierge, business services, meeting room. AE, D, MC, V.*

$$$-$$$$ WAIKĪKĪ PARC. Billed as an executive boutique hotel and owned ★ by the same group that manages the Halekūlani across the street, where guests have signing privileges, the Parc offers the same attention to detail in service and architectural design but lacks a beachfront location. The lobby is light and airy, and guest rooms are done in cool blues and whites and lots of rattan. *2233 Helumoa Rd., Waikīkī, Honolulu 96815, tel. 808/921–7272 or 800/422–0450, fax 808/931–6638, www.waikikiparc.com. 298 rooms. 2 restaurants, room service, in-room safes, minibars, pool, gym, concierge, business services. AE, D, DC, MC, V.*

$$$ ILIMA HOTEL. This 17-story condominium-style hotel has large studios with two double beds and full kitchens; you can also opt for a suite with a spacious lānai. On a side street near the Ala Wai Canal, the Ilima is a short walk away from the International Market Place and the Royal Hawaiian Shopping Center. *445 Nohonani St., Waikīkī, Honolulu 96815, tel. 808/923–1877 or 888/864–5462, fax 808/ 924–8371, www.ilima.com. 99 units. Kitchenettes, pool, sauna. AE, DC, MC, V.*

$$$ OHANA EAST. Formerly the Outrigger East, this hotel is the flagship property for Ohana Hotels in Waikīkī, and is located just two blocks from the beach and a quarter mile from Kapiolani Park. Guests can choose from standard hotel rooms to suites with kitchenettes. *150 Kaiulani Ave., Waikīkī, Honolulu 96815, tel. 808/922– 5353 or 800/462–6262, fax 808/926–4334, www.ohanahotels.com. 423 rooms and suites. 4 restaurants, room service, in-room data ports, refrigerators, pool, fitness room, hair salon, bar, laundry facilities. AE, D, DC, MC, V.*

$$$ QUEEN KAPIʻOLANI HOTEL. This 19-story hotel a half block from the beach appeals to those in search of clean, basic accommodations within walking distance of the water and Waikīkī's main attractions. Some rooms have kitchenettes, and there's a large pool and sundeck on the third floor. *150 Kapahulu Ave., Waikīkī, Honolulu 96815, tel. 808/922–1941 or 800/367–5004, fax 808/922–2694, www.castle-group.com. 308 rooms, 7 suites. 2 restaurants, room service, refrigerators, pool, bar, meeting room. AE, D, DC, MC, V.*

$$$ ROYAL GARDEN AT WAIKĪKĪ. From the outside, this 25-story boutique hotel looks like the average Waikīkī high-rise. But step inside and it whispers elegance, from the marble and etched glass in the lobby to the genuine graciousness of the staff. Guest rooms have sitting areas, private lānai, and marble and brass baths. 440 'Olohana St., Waikīkī, Honolulu 96815, tel. 808/943–0202 or 800/367–5666, fax 808/946–8777, www.royalgardens.com. 202 rooms, 18 suites. 2 restaurants, room service, in-room safes, refrigerators, 2 pools, gym, lobby lounge, business services, meeting room. AE, D, DC, MC, V.

$$$ WAIKĪKĪ JOY. This boutique hotel is a lesser-known gem. The location is great, tucked away on a quiet side street yet still close to Waikīkī's restaurants, shops, and entertainment. Units have either ocean or partial ocean views. Each has a lānai, a whirlpool bath, a deluxe stereo system, and a control panel by the bed. 320 Lewers St., Waikīkī, Honolulu 96815, tel. 808/923–2300 or 800/922–7866, fax 808/924–4010, www.aston-hotels.com. 50 rooms, 44 suites. Kitchenettes, minibars, pool, sauna, lobby lounge. AE, D, DC, MC, V.

$$–$$$ ASTON COCONUT PLAZA HOTEL. With its small size and intimate service, Coconut Plaza, on the Ala Wai Canal and three blocks from the beach, is a true boutique hotel. Tropical plantation decor features rattan furnishings and floral bedspreads. Guest rooms have private lānai, and all except standard-view rooms come with kitchenettes. 450 Lewers St., Waikīkī, Honolulu 96815, tel. 808/923–8828 or 800/882–9696, fax 808/923–3473, www.aston-hotels.com. 70 rooms, 11 suites. Kitchenettes, pool, laundry facilities, meeting room. AE, D, DC, MC, V.

$$–$$$ THE BREAKERS. The Breakers' six two-story buildings surround the pool and overlook gardens filled with tropical flowers. A throwback to the early 1960s, guest rooms have Japanese-style shoji doors. Rooms come with kitchenettes, bath with shower only, and lānai. Guests return here year after year to soak up the laid-back Old Hawaiʻi atmosphere. It's a half block from the beach and from Waikīkī restaurants. *250 Beach Walk, Waikīkī, Honolulu 96815, tel. 808/923–3181 or 800/426–0494, fax 808/923–7174, www. breakers-hawaii.com. 64 units. Kitchenettes, pool. AE, DC, MC, V.*

$$ DIAMOND HEAD BED AND BREAKFAST. The two guest rooms at this bed-and-breakfast on the southeastern edge of Kapiʻolani Park are big, have private baths, and open to a lānai and large backyard that makes the hustle and bustle of Waikīkī seem miles away. Hostess Joanne Trotter has filled the large living spaces with modern artwork and furnishings created for tropical comfort. A minimum two-night stay is required. *3240 Noela Dr., Waikīkī, Honolulu 96815, tel. 808/885–4550, fax 808/885–0559. Reservations: Hawaiʻi's Best Bed and Breakfasts, Box 563, Kamuela, 96743, tel. 808/ 885–4550 or 800/262–9912, fax 808/885–0559, www.bestbnb.com. 2 rooms. No air-conditioning, no room phones. No credit cards.*

$$ HAWAIIANA HOTEL. Step back in time to Old Hawaiʻi at this
★ intimate, low-rise hideaway a few blocks from the beach. The Hawaiiana is surrounded by a garden of tropical plants, and a giant tiki god carving greets you at the entry. The hotel's centerpiece is the pool, and every morning guests are served Kona coffee here. Each room has both a double and single bed as well as a kitchenette and view of the gardens below. *260 Beach Walk, Waikīkī, Honolulu 96815, tel. 808/923–3811 or 800/367–5122, fax 808/926–5728, www.hawaiianahotelwaikiki.com. 95 rooms. Pool, laundry facilities. AE, D, DC, MC, V.*

$$ WAIKĪKĪ HĀNA. Smack dab in the middle of Waikīkī and a block away from the beach, this eight-story hotel is convenient for exploring just about every shop, restaurant, and activity in Oʻahu's tourist hub. Accommodations are clean and plain. Many rooms have their own lānai. Pay a little extra per day and you can rent a refrigerator. *2424 Koa Ave., Waikīkī, Honolulu 96815, tel. 808/926– 8841 or 800/367–5004, fax 808/596–0158, www.castleresorts.com. 70 rooms, 2 suites. Restaurant, in-room safes, kitchenettes, lobby lounge, laundry facilities. AE, DC, MC, V.*

$$ WAIKĪKĪ SAND VILLA. Three blocks from the beach across from the Ala Wai Canal, the Villa's rooms are definitely on the small side but are clean and fairly comfortable. Complimentary breakfast is served daily in the hotel's breakfast room or at tables outside by the swimming pool. Studio accommodations are also available. *2375 Ala Wai Blvd, Waikīkī, Honolulu 96815, tel. 808/922–4744 or 800/ 247–1903, fax 808/923–2541, www.sandvillahotel.com. 212 rooms. Restaurant, refrigerators, pool, hot tub, bar, shop. AE, D, DC, MC, V.*

$ EDMUNDS HOTEL APARTMENTS. Long lānai wrap around the building, so each room has its own view of the pretty Ala Wai Canal and glorious Mānoa Valley beyond—views that look especially lovely at night, when lights are twinkling up in the mountain ridges. This has been a budget alternative for decades, and if you can put up with the constant sounds of traffic on the boulevard, this is a real bargain. The ocean is four blocks away. *2411 Ala Wai Blvd., Waikīkī, Honolulu 96815, tel. 808/923–8381 or 808/732–5169. 8 rooms. Kitchenettes; no air-conditioning. No credit cards.*

$ ROYAL GROVE HOTEL. This flamingo-pink family-oriented hotel is reminiscent of Miami. With just six floors, it is one of Waikīkī's smaller hotels. The lobby is comfortable; the rooms, though agreeably furnished, have neither themes nor views. Go for the high-end rooms if possible; economy rooms have no air-conditioning and more street noise. The hotel is about two blocks from the beach. *15 Uluniu Ave., Waikīkī, Honolulu 96815, tel. 808/923– 7691, fax 808/922–7508. 78 rooms, 7 suites. Kitchenettes, pool; no air-conditioning in some rooms. AE, D, DC, MC, V.*

HONOLULU

$$$$ KĀHALA MANDARIN ORIENTAL HAWAI'I. Minutes away from
★ Waikīkī, on the quiet side of Diamond Head, this elegant oceanfront hotel is hidden in the wealthy neighborhood of Kāhala. Rooms combine touches of Asia and Old Hawai'i, with mahogany furniture, teak parquet floors, hand-loomed area rugs, local art,

and grass-cloth wall coverings. 5000 Kāhala Ave., Kāhala, Honolulu 96816, tel. 808/739–8888 or 800/367–2525, fax 808/739–8800, www.mandarin-oriental.com. 341 rooms, 29 suites. 3 restaurants, room service, minibars, pool, outdoor hot tub, gym, sauna, steam room, beach, dive shop, snorkeling, lobby lounge, concierge, business services, meeting room. AE, D, DC, MC, V.

$$$–$$$$ ALA MOANA HOTEL. This long-standing landmark has an excellent location near the popular Ala Moana Shopping Center (they're connected by a pedestrian ramp), the Hawai'i Convention Center, and Ala Moana Beach Park. Each room in this 36-story high-rise has a lānai with a view of Ala Moana Beach, the ocean, or the mountains. 410 Atkinson Dr., Ala Moana 96814, tel. 808/955–4811 or 888/367–4811, fax 808/944–6839, www.alamoanahotel.com. 1,150 rooms, 67 suites. 4 restaurants, room service, in-room safes, minibars, pool, gym, bar, 2 lobby lounges, dance club, meeting room. AE, DC, MC, V.

$$$–$$$$ ASTON AT THE EXECUTIVE CENTRE HOTEL. Here's a great option for the corporate traveler who wants to avoid Waikīkī. Downtown Honolulu's only hotel is an all-suite high-rise in the center of the business district, within walking distance of the Aloha Tower Marketplace and 10 minutes from Honolulu International Airport. Suites are on the top 10 floors of a 40-story glass-walled tower, providing views of downtown and Honolulu Harbor. Each unit has a separate living area and kitchenette. 1088 Bishop St., Downtown Honolulu 96813, tel. 808/539–3000 or 800/922–7866, fax 808/523–1088, www.aston-hotels.com. 116 suites. Restaurant, in-room safes, kitchenettes, pool, gym, business services, meeting room. AE, DC, MC, V.

$$–$$$ MĀNOA VALLEY INN. An intimate surprise is tucked away in Mānoa Valley, just 2 mi from Waikīkī. Built in 1919, this stately home is on the National Register of Historic Places. Rooms are furnished in country-inn style, with antique four-poster beds, marble-top dressers, patterned wallpaper, and fresh flowers. There's a reading room with a TV and VCR. The separate carriage house sleeps four. 2001 Vancouver Dr., Mānoa, Honolulu 96822, tel. 808/947–6019 or 800/634–5115, fax 808/922–2421. 8 rooms, 4 with bath; 1 house. AE, DC, MC, V.

$$–$$$ PAGODA HOTEL. The location and moderate rates make this a good choice if you're simply looking for a place to sleep and catch a couple of meals. Studios include a full-size refrigerator, a stove, and cooking utensils. There are no memorable views because the hotel is surrounded by high-rises. The floating restaurant is notable for its Japanese gardens and carp-filled waterways. 1525 Rycroft St., Ala Moana, Honolulu 96814, tel. 808/941–6611 or 800/472–4632, fax 808/955–5067, www.hthcorp.com. 364 rooms. 2 restaurants, refrigerators, pool. AE, D, DC, MC, V.

In This Chapter

Updated by Maggie Wunsch

side trips
around oʻahu

A TRIP AROUND OʻAHU BRINGS YOU FACE-TO-FACE with its sheer natural beauty. Roll past the wave-dashed eastern shore, with its photogenic beaches and cliffs. Drive through the central plains past acres of red soil, once rich in pineapple and now supporting diversified crops, such as coffee. Head to the North Shore, a reflection of old Oʻahu with its rickety storefronts and trees hanging heavy with bananas and papaya.

THE EAST OʻAHU RING

At once historic and contemporary, serene and active, the east end of Oʻahu holds within its relatively small area remarkable variety and picture-perfect scenery featuring windswept cliffs and wave-dashed shores.

SIGHTS TO SEE

❼ HĀLONA BLOWHOLE. Below a scenic turnout along the Koko Head shoreline, this oft-photographed lava tube that sucks the ocean in and spits it out in lofty plumes may or may not perform, depending on the currents. Nearby is the tiny beach used to film the wave-washed love scene in *From Here to Eternity*. This beach is not recommended for swimming or even wading. Also, take your valuables with you and lock your car, because it's a hot spot for petty thieves. *Kalanianaʻole Hwy., 1 mi east of Hanauma Bay.*

⑥ MAKAPU'U POINT. This spot has breathtaking views of the ocean, mountains, and the windward islands. The peninsula jutting out in the distance is **Mōkapu,** site of a U.S. Marine base. The spired mountain peak is **Mt. Olomana.** In front of you on the long pier is part of the **Makai Undersea Test Range,** a research facility that is closed to the public. Offshore is **Rabbit Island,** a picturesque cay so named because some think it looks like a swimming bunny.

Nestled in the cliff face is the **Makapu'u Lighthouse,** which is closed to the public. Near the Makapu'u Point turnout, you'll find the start of a mile-long paved road (closed to traffic). Hike up it to the top of the 647-ft bluff for a closer view of the lighthouse and, during the winter months, a great whale-watching vantage point. *Kalaniana'ole Hwy., turnout above Makapu'u Beach.*

❶ NU'UANU PALI LOOKOUT. This panoramic perch looks out to windward O'ahu. It was in this region that King Kamehameha I drove defending forces over the edges of the 1,000-ft-high cliffs, thus winning the decisive battle for control of O'ahu. Lock your car if you get out, because break-ins have occurred here. *Top of Pali Hwy.*

❷ QUEEN EMMA SUMMER PALACE. Queen Emma and her family used this stately white home, built in 1848, as a retreat from the rigors of court life in hot and dusty Honolulu during the mid-1800s. *2913 Pali Hwy., tel. 808/595-3167. $5. Guided tours daily 9–4.*

❺ SEA LIFE PARK. Dolphins leap and spin, penguins frolic, and a killer whale performs impressive tricks at the shows in this marine-life attraction. Inquire about the park's behind-the-scenes tour for a glimpse of dolphin-training areas and the seabird rehabilitation center. *Kalaniana'ole Hwy., Waimānalo, tel. 808/259–7933, www.atlantisadventures.com. $24. Daily 9:30–5.*

❸ ULUPŌ HEIAU. Though they may look like piles of rocks to the uninitiated, *heiau* are sacred stone platforms for the worship of the gods and date from ancient times. Ulupō means "night inspiration," referring to the legendary *menehune*, a mythical race of diminutive people who supposedly built the heiau under the cloak of darkness. *Behind YMCA at Kalaniana'ole Hwy. and Kailua Rd.*

 WAIMĀNALO. This modest little seaside town flanked by chiseled cliffs is worth a visit. Its biggest draw is its beautiful beach, offering glorious views to the windward side. Down the side roads, heading mauka, are little farms that grow a variety of fruits and flowers. Toward the back of the valley are small ranches with grazing horses. *Kalaniana'ole Hwy.*

WHERE TO EAT

$$ BUZZ'S ORIGINAL STEAKHOUSE. This family-owned restaurant is just across the road from Kailua Beach Park and epitomizes the kind of laid-back style you'd expect to find in Hawai'i. Burgers, salads, and fresh fish sandwiches are the lunch staples. *413 Kawailoa Rd., tel. 808/261–4661. No credit cards.*

$$ ROY'S. Two walls of windows offer views of Maunalua Bay and Diamond Head in the distance. Dishes with a modern flair— blackened 'ahi in a hot, soy-mustard butter sauce—share the menu with comfort-food favorites, such as meat loaf with mushroom gravy. *Hawai'i Kai Corporate Plaza, 6600 Kalaniana'ole Hwy., tel. 808/396–7697. AE, D, DC, MC, V.*

$ BUENO NALO. The owners of this family-run eatery are dedicated to healthful Mexican cuisine, and the food is reliably good. Combination plates with tacos, enchiladas, and tamales are bargains. Velvet paintings and piñatas add a fun, funky flavor to the setting. *20 Kainehe St., tel. 808/263–1999. AE, MC, V.*

AROUND THE ISLAND

After visiting populated West Honolulu, you'll find that the O'ahu landscape turns increasingly rural as you head north. Once carpeted in pineapple and sugarcane plantations, the

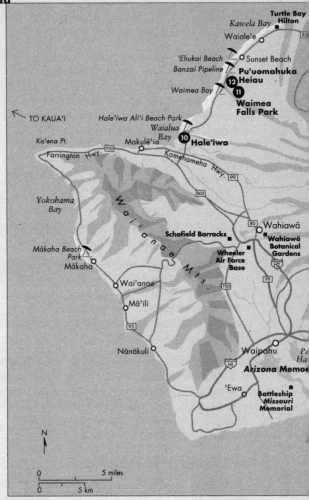

Turtle Bay Hilton

Kawela Bay

Waiale'e

83

'Ehukai Beach ○ Sunset Beach

Banzai Pipeline **Pu'uomahuka Heiau**

12

Waimea Bay **11**

Waimea Falls Park

← TO KAUA'I

Hale'iwa Ali'i Beach Park

Ka'ena Pt. *Waialua Bay*

Mokulē'ia **10** **Hale'iwa**

Farrington Hwy. 930 *Kamehameha Hwy.* 99

803

Yokohama Bay

W a i a n a e

80 Wahiawā

Schofield Barracks **Wahiawā Botanical Gardens**

Mākaha Beach Park **Wheeler Air Force Base** H2

Mākaha *M t s.* 750 99

○ Wai'anae

○ Mā'ili

93

○ Nānākuli

Waipahu

H1

Arizona Memor

'Ewa

Battleship Missouri Memorial

N

0   5 miles

0   5 km

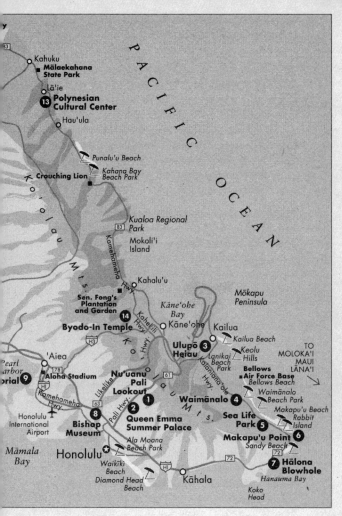

central plains and the North Shore are now home to ranches, banana farms, and fields of exotic flowers and coffee grown for export.

SIGHTS TO SEE

★ ❾ **ARIZONA MEMORIAL.** A simple, gleaming white structure shields the hulk of the U.S.S. Arizona, which sank with 1,102 men aboard when the Japanese attacked Pearl Harbor on December 7, 1941. Appropriate dress is required (no bathing suits, slippers, or bare feet). *National Park Service, Pearl Harbor, tel. 808/422–0561 or 808/423–2263, www.nps.gov/usar. Free. Tour tickets distributed on a first-come, first-served basis, with 1- to 3-hr waits common. Daily 8–3.*

BATTLESHIP MISSOURI MEMORIAL. The U.S.S. Missouri saw action from World War II to the Persian Gulf War, and on these decks the agreement for Japanese surrender to end World War II was signed. The famed battleship, now moored about 1,000 ft from the Arizona, serves as a museum and interactive educational center. *Pearl Harbor, tel. 808/423–2263 or 888/877–6477, www.ussmissouri.com. $14, guided tours $20. Daily 9–5.*

❽ **BISHOP MUSEUM.** Founded in 1889 by Charles R. Bishop as a memorial to his wife, Princess Bernice Pauahi, the museum began as a repository for the royal possessions of this last direct descendant of King Kamehameha the Great. Today it is the Hawai'i State Museum of Natural and Cultural History, with world-famous displays of Polynesian artifacts. *1525 Bernice St., tel. 808/847–3511, www.bishophawaii.org. $14.95. Daily 9–5.*

❶❹ **BYODO-IN TEMPLE.** Tucked away in the back of the Valley of the Temples cemetery is a replica of the 11th-century Temple at Uji in Japan. A 2-ton statue of the Buddha presides inside the main temple building and alongside a meditation house and gardens set dramatically against the sheer, green cliffs of the Ko'olau Mountains. *47-200 Kahekili Hwy., Kāne'ohe, tel. 808/239–8811. $2. Daily 8–4:30.*

⑩ HALEʻIWA. During the 1920s this seaside hamlet was a trendy retreat at the end of a railroad line. During the '60s hippies gathered here, followed by surfers. Today Haleʻiwa is a fun mix, with old general stores and contemporary boutiques, galleries, and eateries. *Follow H-1 west from Honolulu to H-2 north, exit at Wahiawā, follow Kamehameha Hwy. 6 mi, turn left at signaled intersection, then right into Haleʻiwa.*

 ⑬ POLYNESIAN CULTURAL CENTER. Re-created, individual villages showcase the lifestyles and traditions of Hawaiʻi, Tahiti, Samoa, Fiji, the Marquesas Islands, New Zealand, and Tonga. This 45-acre center, founded in 1963 by the Church of Jesus Christ of Latter-day Saints, also houses restaurants and lūʻaus, and shares cultural traditions such as tribal tattooing, fire dancing, and ancient customs and ceremonies. *55-370 Kamehameha Hwy., Lāʻie, tel. 808/293–3333, www.polynesia.com. $35–$125. Mon.–Sat. 12:30–9:30.*

⑫ PUʻUOMAHUKA HEIAU. Worth a stop for its spectacular views from a bluff high above the ocean overlooking Waimea Bay, this sacred spot was once the site of human sacrifices. *½ mi north of Waimea Bay on Rte. 83, turn right on Pūpūkea Rd. and drive 1 mi uphill.*

⑪ WAIMEA FALLS PARK. At this 1,800-acre attraction, remnants of an early Hawaiian civilization are surrounded by more than 2,500 tropical plants and trees. There's a spectacular show of cliff-diving from 45-ft-high falls. Tour the backcountry on horseback or by kayak, mountain bike, or all-terrain vehicle. *59-864 Kamehameha Hwy., Haleʻiwa, tel. 808/638–8511, www.atlantisadventures.com. $24. Daily 10–5:30.*

WHERE TO EAT

$–$$ HALEIWA JOE'S. A day of surfing or just watching the big wave riders can work up an appetite. Haleiwa Joe's, located just past the Anahulu Stream Bridge, serves up steaks, prime rib, and seafood, such as crunchy coconut shrimp and grilled salmon with Asian pesto sauce. Come in time to watch the sun set over

Hotel How-Tos

Where you stay does make a difference. Do you prefer a modern high-rise or an intimate B&B? A center-city location or the quiet suburbs? What facilities do you want? Sort through your priorities, then price it all out.

HOW TO GET A DEAL After you've chosen a likely candidate or two, phone them directly and price a room for your travel dates. Then call the hotel's toll-free number and ask the same questions. Also try consolidators and hotel-room discounters. You won't hear the same rates twice. On the spot, make a reservation as soon as you are quoted a price you want to pay.

PROMISES, PROMISES If you have special requests, make them when you reserve. Get written confirmation of any promises.

SETTLE IN Upon arriving, make sure everything works—lights and lamps, TV and radio, sink, tub, shower, and anything else that matters. Report any problems immediately. And don't wait until you need extra pillows or blankets or an ironing board to call housekeeping. Also check out the fire emergency instructions. Know where to find the fire exits, and make sure your companions do, too.

IF YOU NEED TO COMPLAIN Be polite but firm. Explain the problem to the person in charge. Suggest a course of action. If you aren't satisfied, repeat your requests to the manager. Document everything: Take pictures and keep a written record of who you've spoken with, when, and what was said. Contact your travel agent, if he made the reservations.

KNOW THE SCORE When you go out, take your hotel's business cards (one for everyone in your party). If you have extras, you can give them out to new acquaintances who want to call you.

TIP UP FRONT For special services, a tip or partial tip in advance can work wonders.

USE ALL THE HOTEL RESOURCES A concierge can make difficult things easy. But a desk clerk, bellhop, or other hotel employee who's friendly, smart, and ambitious can often steer you straight as well. A gratuity is in order if the advice is helpful.

Hale'iwa Harbor. *66-0011 Kamehameha Hwy., tel. 808/637–8005. Reservations not accepted. AE, DC, MC, V.*

$ KUA 'AINA SANDWICH. A must-stop spot during a drive around the island, this tiny North Shore eatery has a few tables inside and a few more on the lānai next to the road. Try the grilled mahimahi sandwich. You can also check out Kua 'Aina's south shore location across from the Ward Centre in Honolulu. *66-214 Kamehameha Hwy., tel. 808/637–6067. Reservations not accepted. No credit cards.*

practical information

Air Travel

Most flights to Honolulu International originate in Los Angeles or San Francisco, which means they are nonstop. Flying time from the West Coast is 4½–5 hours. Honolulu also has a number of carriers routing to the islands from the United Kingdom.

CARRIERS
Carriers flying into Honolulu from the mainland United States include American, Continental, Delta, Hawaiian, Northwest, and United. Carriers flying from the United Kingdom to Honolulu include Air New Zealand, American, Continental, Delta, and United. Rates for an APEX ticket vary. Check around for the best offer.

Charter flights are the least expensive and the least reliable—with chronically late departures and occasional cancellations. They also tend to depart less frequently (usually once a week) than do regularly scheduled flights. The savings may be worth the potential annoyance, however. Charter flights serving Honolulu International Airport are available from American Trans Air and Hawaiian Airlines.

➤AIRLINES AND CONTACTS: Air New Zealand (tel. 800/262–1234, www.aimz.com). American (tel. 808/833–7600 or 800/433–7300, www.aa.com). American Trans Air (tel. 800/225–2995, www.ata.com). Continental (tel. 800/523–3273, www.continental.com). Delta (tel. 800/221–1212, www.delta.com).

Hawaiian Airlines (tel. 808/838–1555 or 800/367–5320, www.hawaiianair.com). **Northwest** (tel. 808/955–2255 or 800/225–2525, www.nwa.com). **United** (tel. 800/241–6522, www.ual.com).

CHECK-IN & BOARDING

Always ask your carrier about its check-in policy. Plan to arrive at the airport about two hours before your scheduled departure time for domestic flights and 2¼ to 3 hours before international flights. Plan to arrive at the airport 45 minutes to 60 minutes before departure for interisland flights.

Prior to check-in, all luggage being taken out of Hawai'i must pass agricultural inspection. Fruit, plants, and processed foods that have been labeled and packed for export (including pineapples, papaya, coconuts, flowers, and macadamia nuts) are permitted. Fresh fruit and other agricultural items, including seed leis, are not, and will be confiscated.

FLYING TIMES

Flying time is about 10 hours from New York, 8 hours from Chicago, 5 hours from Los Angeles, and 15 hours from London, not including layovers.

Airports and Transfers

AIRPORTS

More direct flights, by more domestic and international air carriers, arrive and depart from Honolulu International than at any other airport in Hawai'i.

➤**AIRPORT INFORMATION: Honolulu International Airport** (tel. 808/836–6411, www.ehawaiigov.org). **Pacific Aerospace Museum** (tel. 808/839–0777, $3).

AIRPORT TRANSFERS

There are taxis right at the airport baggage-claim exit. At $1.50 start-up plus $1.50 for each mile, the fare to Waikīkī will run approximately $23, plus tip. Drivers are also allowed to charge

30¢ per suitcase. Trans Hawaiian Services runs an airport shuttle service to Waikīkī. The fare is $8 one-way, $15 round-trip. The municipal bus (TheBus) will take you into Waikīkī for only $1.50, but you are allowed only one bag, which must fit on your lap. Some hotels have their own pickup service. Check when you book.

➤TAXIS AND SHUTTLES: TheBus (tel. 808/848–5555, www.thebus.org). Trans Hawaiian Services (tel. 808/566–7333).

Business Hours

Even people in paradise have to work. Local business hours are generally 8 to 5 weekdays. Bigger malls stay open until 9 weekdays and Saturday and close at 5 on Sunday. Boutiques in resort areas may stay open as late as 11. Banks are usually open Monday through Thursday 8:30 to 3 and until 6 on Friday. Some banks have Saturday morning hours.

Most museums generally open their doors between 9 AM and 10 AM and stay open until 5 PM Tuesday through Saturday.

Bus Travel

You can go all around the island or just down Kalākaua Avenue for $1.50 on Honolulu's municipal transportation system, affectionately known as TheBus. You're entitled to one free transfer per fare if you ask for it when boarding. Exact change is required, and dollar bills are accepted. A four-day pass for visitors costs $10 and is sold at the more than 30 ABC stores (Hawaiian chain stores that sell sundries and are geared to tourists) in Waikīkī. Monthly passes cost $25.

There are no official bus-route maps, but you can find privately published booklets at most drugstores and other convenience outlets. The important route numbers for Waikīkī are 2, 4, 8, 19, 20, and 58. If you venture afield, you can always get back on one of these.

There are also a number of brightly painted private buses, many free, that will take you to such commercial attractions as dinner cruises, garment factories, and the like.

➤**BUS INFORMATION: TheBus** (tel. 808/848–5555, www.thebus. org).

Car Rental

If you plan to go beyond Waikīkī to tour Oʻahu, renting a car is essential. During peak seasons—summer, Christmas vacations, and February—reservations are necessary. Rental agencies abound in and around the Honolulu International Airport and in Waikīkī. Local agencies rent everything from used cars to classics and pickup trucks. Rates in Honolulu begin at $38 a day ($164 a week) for an economy car with air-conditioning, automatic transmission, and unlimited mileage.

Cloud Nine Limousine Service provides red-carpet treatment in its chauffeur-driven superstretch limousines. Rates begin at $60 an hour, plus tax and tip, with a two-hour minimum. Another reliable company is Duke's Limousine Service, which offers a choice of luxury superstretches, sedans, or SUV limousines, with rates that begin at $45 per hour, with a two-hour minimum.

➤**MAJOR AGENCIES: Avis** (tel. 808/834–5536 or 800/321–3712, www.avis.com). **Budget** (tel. 800/527–0700; 800/527–7000 in Hawaiʻi, www.budget.com). **Dollar** (tel. 808/831–2330 or 800/800–4000, www.dollarcar.com). **Enterprise** (tel. 808/836–7722 or 800/736–8222, www.enterprise.com). **Hertz** (tel. 808/831–3500 or 800/654–3011, www.hertz.com). **National** (tel. 808/831–3800 or 800/227–7368, www.nationalcar.com). **Thrifty** (tel. 808/831–2277 or 800/367–2277).

➤**LOCAL AGENCIES: JN Car and Truck Rentals** (tel. 808/831–2724). **Paradise Rent A Car** (tel. 808/946–7777 or 888/882–2277, www.paradiserentacar.com). **VIP** (tel. 808/922–4605).

➤**LIMOUSINE RENTALS: Cloud Nine Limousine Service** (tel. 808/524–7999 or 800/524–7999). **Duke's Limousine, Inc.** (tel. 808/738–1878, www.dukeslimo.com).

REQUIREMENTS & RESTRICTIONS

In Hawai'i you must be 21 years of age to rent a car and you must have a valid driver's license and a major credit card. Those under 25 will pay a daily surcharge of $15.

In Hawai'i your unexpired mainland driver's license is valid for rental up to 90 days.

SURCHARGES

Before you pick up a car in one city and leave it in another, **ask about drop-off charges or one-way service fees,** which can be substantial. Note, too, that some rental agencies charge extra if you return the car before the time specified in your contract. To avoid a hefty refueling fee, **fill the tank just before you turn in the car,** but be aware that gas stations near the rental outlet may overcharge. It's almost never a deal to buy the tank of gas in the car when you rent it; the understanding is that you'll return it empty, but some fuel usually remains. Surcharges may apply if you're under 25. You'll pay extra for child seats (about $6 a day), which are compulsory for children under five, and for additional drivers (about $5 per day).

Car Travel

O'ahu's drivers are generally courteous, and you rarely hear a horn. People will slow down and let you into traffic with a wave of the hand. A friendly wave back is customary. If a driver sticks a hand out the window in a fist with the thumb and pinky sticking straight out, this is a good thing: the Hawaiian symbol for "hang loose," it's called the *shaka* and is often used to say "thanks," as well.

Hawai'i has a seat-belt law for front-seat passengers and those under the age of 18 in the back seats. Children under 40 pounds must be in a car seat, available from your car-rental agency.

Driving in rush-hour traffic (6:30–8:30 and 3:30–5:30) can be exasperating because left turns are prohibited at many intersections. Parking along many streets is curtailed during these hours, and towing is strictly enforced. Read the curbside parking signs before leaving your vehicle, even at a meter. Remember not to leave valuables in your car. Rental cars are often targets for thieves.

RULES OF THE ROAD

The highway speed limit is usually 55 mph. In-town traffic moves from 25 to 40 mph. Jaywalking is very common, so be particularly watchful for pedestrians, especially in congested areas such as Waikīkī. Unauthorized use of a parking space reserved for persons with disabilities can net you a $150 fine.

Asking for directions will almost always produce a helpful explanation from the locals, but you should be prepared for an island term or two. Instead of using compass directions, remember that Hawai'i residents refer to places as being either *mauka* (toward the mountains) or *makai* (toward the ocean) from one another. Other directions depend on your location: in Honolulu, for example, people say to "go Diamond Head," which means toward that famous landmark, or to "go 'ewa," meaning in the opposite direction. A shop on the mauka–Diamond Head corner of a street is on the mountain side of the street on the corner closest to Diamond Head. It all makes perfect sense once you get the lay of the land.

Children in Hawai'i

Sunny beaches and many family-oriented cultural sites, activities, and attractions make Hawai'i a very *keiki*- (child-) friendly place. Here kids can swim with a dolphin, surf with a boogie board, check out an active volcano, or ride a sugarcane train. Parents should **use caution on beaches and during water sports.** Even waters that appear calm can harbor powerful rip currents. Be sure to **read any beach warning guides your hotel may provide. Ask around for kid-friendly beaches** that might have shallow tidal pools or are protected by reefs. And remember that the sun's rays are in operation full-force year-round here. Sunblock for children is essential.

SIGHTS & ATTRACTIONS

Top picks for children run the gamut from natural attractions kids can enjoy for free to some fairly expensive amusements. On O'ahu, favorites include hiking Diamond Head, snorkeling Hanauma Bay, learning about marine life at Sea Life Park, playing ancient Hawaiian games at Waimea Valley Adventures Park, and touring through South Pacific cultures at the Polynesian Cultural Center.

Places that are especially appealing to children are indicated by a rubber-duckie icon (🐥) in the margin.

Customs & Duties

When shopping, **keep receipts** for all purchases. Upon reentering your country or the mainland, **be ready to show customs officials what you've bought.** If you feel a duty is incorrect or object to the way your clearance was handled, note the inspector's badge number and ask to see a supervisor. If the problem isn't resolved, write to the appropriate authorities, beginning with the port director at your point of entry.

IN AUSTRALIA

Australian residents who are 18 or older may bring home A$400 worth of souvenirs and gifts (including jewelry), 250 cigarettes or 250 grams of tobacco, and 1,125 ml of alcohol (including wine, beer, and spirits). Residents under 18 may bring back

A$200 worth of goods. Prohibited items include meat products. Seeds, plants, and fruits need to be declared upon arrival.

➤**INFORMATION: AUSTRALIAN CUSTOMS SERVICE** (Regional Director, Box 8, Sydney, NSW 2001, tel. 02/9213–2000, fax 02/9213–4000, www.customs.gov.au).

IN CANADA

Canadian residents who have been out of Canada for at least seven days may bring in C$750 worth of goods duty-free. If you've been away fewer than seven days but more than 48 hours, the duty-free allowance drops to C$200; if your trip lasts 24 to 48 hours, the allowance is C$50. You may not pool allowances with family members. Goods claimed under the C$750 exemption may follow you by mail; those claimed under the lesser exemptions must accompany you. Alcohol and tobacco products may be included in the seven-day and 48-hour exemptions but not in the 24-hour exemption. If you meet the age requirements of the province or territory through which you reenter Canada, you may bring in, duty-free, 1.5 liters of wine or 1.14 liters (40 imperial ounces) of liquor or 24 12-ounce cans or bottles of beer or ale. If you are 19 or older you may bring in, duty-free, 200 cigarettes and 50 cigars. Check ahead of time with the Canada Customs and Revenue Agency or the Department of Agriculture for policies regarding meat products, seeds, plants, and fruits.

You may send an unlimited number of gifts (only one gift per recipient, however) worth up to C$60 each duty-free to Canada. Label the package UNSOLICITED GIFT—VALUE UNDER $60. Alcohol and tobacco are excluded.

➤**INFORMATION: Canada Customs and Revenue Agency** (2265 St. Laurent Blvd. S, Ottawa, Ontario K1G 4K3, tel. 204/983–3500; 506/636–5064; 800/461–9999 in Canada, www.ccra-adrc.gc.ca).

IN HAWAI'I

Plants and plant products are subject to regulation by the Department of Agriculture, both on entering and leaving Hawai'i. Upon leaving the Islands, you'll have to have your bags x-rayed and tagged at one of the airport's agricultural inspection stations before you proceed to check-in. Pineapples and coconuts with the packer's agricultural inspection stamp pass freely; papayas must be treated, inspected, and stamped. All other fruits are banned for export to the U.S. mainland. Flowers pass except for gardenia, rose leaves, jade vine, and mauna loa. Also banned are insects, snails, soil, cotton, cacti, sugarcane, and all berry plants.

You'll have to **leave dogs and other pets at home.** A strict six-month quarantine is imposed to keep out rabies, which is nonexistent in Hawai'i.

➤**INFORMATION: U.S. Customs Service** (for inquiries, 1300 Pennsylvania Ave. NW, Washington, DC 20229, tel. 202/354–1000, www.customs.gov; for complaints, Customer Satisfaction Unit, 1300 Pennsylvania Ave. NW, Room 5.5A, Washington, DC 20229; for registration of equipment, Office of Passenger Programs, 1300 Pennsylvania Ave. NW, Room 5.4D, Washington, DC 20229, tel. 202/927–0530).

IN NEW ZEALAND

All homeward-bound residents may bring back NZ$700 worth of souvenirs and gifts; passengers may not pool their allowances, and children can claim only the concession on goods intended for their own use. For those 17 or older, the duty-free allowance also includes 4.5 liters of wine or beer; one 1,125-ml bottle of spirits; and either 200 cigarettes, 250 grams of tobacco, 50 cigars, or a combination of the three up to 250 grams. Meat products, seeds, plants, and fruits must be declared upon arrival to the Agricultural Services Department.

➤**INFORMATION: New Zealand Customs** (Head Office, The Customhouse, 17–21 Whitmore St., Box 2218, Wellington, tel. 09/300–5399, www.customs.govt.nz).

IN THE U.K.
From countries outside the European Union, including the United States, you may bring home, duty-free, 200 cigarettes or 50 cigars; 1 liter of spirits or 2 liters of fortified or sparkling wine or liqueurs; 2 liters of still table wine; 60 ml of perfume; 250 ml of toilet water; plus £145 worth of other goods, including gifts and souvenirs. Prohibited items include meat products, seeds, plants, and fruits.

➤**INFORMATION: HM Customs and Excise** (St. Christopher House, Southwark, London SE1 OTE, tel. 020/7928–3344, www.hmce.gov.uk).

Dining
The restaurants we list are the cream of the crop in each price category.

RESERVATIONS & DRESS
Hawai'i is decidedly casual. Aloha shirts and shorts or long pants for men and island-style dresses or casual resort wear for women are standard attire for evenings in most hotel restaurants and local eateries. T-shirts and shorts will do the trick for breakfast and lunch.

Reservations are always a good idea; we mention them only when they're essential or not accepted. Book as far ahead as you can, and reconfirm as soon as you arrive. (Large parties should always call ahead to check the reservations policy.) We mention dress only when men are required to wear a jacket or a jacket and tie.

Disabilities & Accessibility

The Society for the Advancement of Travel for the Handicapped has named Hawai'i the most accessible vacation spot for people with disabilities. Ramped visitor areas and specially equipped lodgings are relatively common. The Hawai'i Center for Independent Living publishes the "Aloha Guide to Accessibility," which lists addresses and telephone numbers for support-service organizations and rates the Islands' hotels, beaches, shopping and entertainment centers, and major attractions. The guide costs $15 but is available in sections for $3 to $5 per section. Part I (general information) is free. Travelers with vision impairments who use a guide dog don't have to worry about quarantine restrictions. All you need to do is present documentation that the animal is a trained guide dog and has a current inoculation record for rabies.

➤**LOCAL RESOURCES: Disability and Communications Access Board** (3060 'Eiwa St., Room 207, Līhu'e, Kaua'i 96766, tel. 808/274–3308; 54 High St., Wailuku, Maui 96793, tel. 808/984–8219). **Hawai'i Center for Independent Living** (414 Kauwili St., Suite 102, Honolulu, O'ahu 96817, tel. 808/522–5400).

SIGHTS & ATTRACTIONS

Many of Hawai'i's sights and attractions are accessible to travelers with disabilities. In Waikīkī, the Honolulu Department of Parks and Recreation can assist in obtaining an "all-terrain" wheelchair for strolls down the beach. Accessibility Vans of Hawaii can help travelers plan activities from snorkeling to whale-watching.

➤**INFORMATION: Accessibility Vans of Hawaii** (tel. 800/303–3750, www.accessiblevanshawaii.com). **Honolulu Department of Parks and Recreation** (Therapeutic Recreation Unit: tel. 808/522–7034).

TRANSPORTATION

Paratransit Services (HandiVan) will take you to a specific destination on Oʻahu—not on sightseeing outings—in vans with lifts and lock-downs. With a HandiVan Pass, one-way trips cost $1.50. Passes are free and can be obtained from the Department of Transportation Services, which is open weekdays from 7:45 to 4:30; you'll need a doctor's written confirmation of your disability or a paratransit ID card. Handi-Cabs of the Pacific also operates ramp-equipped vans with lock-downs in Honolulu. Fares are $9 plus $2.25 per mi for curbside service. Reservations at least one day in advance are required by both companies, so plan ahead.

Those who prefer to do their own driving may rent hand-controlled cars from Avis (reserve 24 hours ahead) and Hertz (24- to 72-hour notice required). You can use the windshield card from your own state to park in spaces reserved for people with disabilities.

➤INFORMATION: **Avis** (tel. 800/331–1212). **Department of Transportation Services** (711 Kapiʻolani Blvd., Honolulu 96819, tel. 808/523–4083). **Handi-Cabs of the Pacific** (tel. 808/524–3866). **Hertz** (tel. 800/654–3131). **Paratransit Services (HandiVan)** (tel. 808/456–5555).

Emergencies

To reach the police, fire department, or an ambulance in an emergency, dial 911.

A doctor, laboratory-radiology technician, and nurses are always on duty at Doctors on Call. Appointments are recommended but not necessary. Dozens of kinds of medical insurance are accepted, including Medicare, Medicaid, and most kinds of travel insurance.

Kūhiō Pharmacy is Waikīkī's only pharmacy and handles prescription requests only until 4:30 PM. Long's Drugs is open evenings at its Ala Moana location and 24 hours at its South King Street location (15 minutes from Waikīkī by car). Pillbox Pharmacy, located in Kaimuki, will deliver prescription medications, for a small fee.

►**DOCTORS AND DENTISTS: Doctors on Call** (Sheraton Princess Kaiulani Hotel, 120 Kaiulani Ave., Waikīkī, tel. 808/971–6000).

►**EMERGENCY SERVICES: Coast Guard Rescue Center** (tel. 800/552–6458).

►**HOSPITALS: Castle Medical Center** (640 Ulukahiki, Kailua, tel. 808/263–5500). **Kapiolani Medical Center for Women and Children** (1319 Punahou St., Honolulu, tel. 808/983–6000). **Queen's Medical Center** (1301 Punchbowl St., Honolulu, tel. 808/538–9011). **Saint Francis Medical Center–West** (91-2141 Ft. Weaver Rd., 'Ewa Beach, tel. 808/678–7000). **Straub Clinic** (888 S. King St., Honolulu, tel. 808/522–4000).

►**PHARMACIES: Kūhiō Pharmacy** (Outrigger West Hotel, 2330 Kūhiō Ave., Waikīkī, tel. 808/923–4466). **Long's Drugs** (Ala Moana Shopping Center, 1450 Ala Moana Blvd., 2nd level, Ala Moana, tel. 808/949–4010; 2220 S. King St., Mō'ili'ili, tel. 808/947–2651). **Pillbox Pharmacy** (1133 11th Ave., Kaimuki, tel. 808/737–1777).

Etiquette & Behavior

In 2003, Hawai'i celebrates 43 years of statehood, so residents can be pretty sensitive to visitors who refer to their own hometowns "back in the States." Remember, **when in Hawai'i, refer to the contiguous 48 states as "the mainland" and not as the United States.** When you do, people will think of you as less of a *malahini* (newcomer).

Gay & Lesbian Travel

A few small hotels and some bed-and-breakfasts in Hawai'i are favored by gay and lesbian visitors; Purple Roofs is a listing agent for gay-friendly accommodations in Hawai'i. In addition, a computerized Gay Community listing compiled by GLEA (Gay & Lesbian Education Advocacy Foundation) is available. Pacific Ocean Holidays specializes in prearranging package tours for independent gay travelers; the organization also publishes the *Pocket Guide to Hawai'i*, distributed free in the state at gay-operated venues and available for $5 by mail for one issue.

For details about the gay and lesbian scene, consult *Fodor's Gay Guide to the USA* (available in bookstores everywhere).

➤**LOCAL RESOURCES: GLEA** (Box 37083, Honolulu 96837, tel. 808/532–9000). **Pacific Ocean Holidays** (Box 88245, Honolulu 96830, tel. 808/923–2400 or 800/735–6600, www.gayHawaii. com). **Purple Roofs** (tel. 925/944–9776, www.purpleroofs.com).

Health

Hawai'i is known as the Health State. The life expectancy here is 79 years, the longest in the nation. Balmy weather makes it easy to remain active year-round, and the low-stress aloha attitude certainly contributes to general well-being. When visiting the Islands, however, there are a few health issues to keep in mind.

The Hawaii State Department of Health recommends that you **drink 16 ounces of water per hour to avoid dehydration when hiking or spending time in the sun. Use sunblock, wear UV-reflective sunglasses, and protect your head with a visor or hat for shade.** If you're not acclimated to warm, humid weather you should allow plenty of time for rest stops and refreshments.

DIVERS' ALERT
Do not fly within 24 hours of scuba diving.

PESTS & OTHER HAZARDS

The Islands have their share of bugs and insects that enjoy the tropical climate as much as visitors do. Most are harmless but annoying. When planning to spend time outdoors in hiking areas, **wear long-sleeved clothing and long pants and use mosquito repellant containing deet.** In very damp places you may encounter the dreaded local centipede. In the Islands they usually come in two colors, brown and blue, and they range from the size of a worm to an 8-inch cigar. Their sting is very painful, and the reaction is similar to bee- and wasp-sting reactions. When camping, **shake out your sleeping bag before climbing in, and check your shoes in the morning,** as the centipedes like cozy places. If planning on hiking or traveling in remote areas, **always carry a first-aid kit and appropriate medications for sting reactions.**

Holidays

Major national holidays include New Year's Day (Jan. 1); Martin Luther King, Jr., Day (3rd Mon. in Jan.); President's Day (3rd Mon. in Feb.); Memorial Day (last Mon. in May); Independence Day (July 4); Labor Day (1st Mon. in Sept.); Thanksgiving Day (4th Thurs. in Nov.); Christmas Eve and Christmas Day (Dec. 24 and 25); and New Year's Eve (Dec. 31).

In addition, Hawai'i celebrates Prince Kuhio Day (Mar. 26); King Kamehameha Day (June 11); and Admission Day (3rd Fri. in Aug.). State, city, and county offices as well as many local companies are closed for business.

For International Travelers

For information on customs restrictions, *see* Customs & Duties.

CAR RENTAL

When picking up a rental car, non-U.S. residents need a reservation voucher for any prepaid reservations that were made in the traveler's home country, a passport, a driver's license, and a travel policy that covers each driver.

CAR TRAVEL

Along larger highways, roadside stops with rest rooms, fast-food restaurants, and sundries stores are well spaced. State police and tow trucks patrol major highways and lend assistance. If your car breaks down on an interstate, pull onto the shoulder and wait for help, or have your passengers wait while you walk to an emergency phone. If you carry a cell phone, dial *55, noting your location on the small green roadside mileage markers.

Driving in the United States is on the right. Do obey speed limits posted along roads and highways. Watch for lower limits in small towns and on back roads.

CONSULATES & EMBASSIES

➤AUSTRALIA: Australian Consulate (1000 Bishop St., Honolulu 96813, tel. 808/524–5050).

➤CANADA: Canadian Consulate (1000 Bishop St., Honolulu 96813, tel. 808/524–5050).

➤NEW ZEALAND: New Zealand Consulate (900 Richards St., Honolulu 96813, tel. 808/543–7900).

➤UNITED KINGDOM: British Consulate General (1000 Bishop St., Honolulu 96813, tel. 808/524–5050).

CURRENCY

The dollar is the basic unit of U.S. currency. It has 100 cents. Coins include the copper penny (1¢); the silvery nickel (5¢), dime (10¢), quarter (25¢), half-dollar (50¢), and the golden $1 coin, replacing a now-rare silver dollar. Bills are denominated $1, $5, $10, $20, $50, and $100, all green and identical in size; designs vary. The exchange rate at press time was US$1.45 per British pound, 66¢ per Canadian dollar, 54¢ per Australian dollar, and 44¢ per New Zealand dollar.

ELECTRICITY

The U.S. standard is AC, 110 volts/60 cycles. Plugs have two flat pins set parallel to each other.

PASSPORTS & VISAS

When traveling internationally, **carry your passport** even if you don't need one (it's always the best form of I.D.) and **make two photocopies of the data page** (one for someone at home and another for you, carried separately from your passport). If you lose your passport, promptly call the nearest embassy or consulate and the local police.

Visas are not necessary for Canadian citizens, or for citizens of Australia and the United Kingdom who are staying fewer than 90 days.

TELEPHONES

All U.S. telephone numbers consist of a three-digit area code and a seven-digit local number. Within most local calling areas, you dial only the seven-digit number. Within the same area code, dial "1" first. To call between area-code regions, dial "1" then all 10 digits; the same goes for calls to numbers prefixed by "800," "888," and "877"—all toll-free. For calls to numbers preceded by "900" you must pay—usually dearly.

For international calls, dial "011" followed by the country code and the local number. For help, dial "0" and ask for an overseas operator. The country code is 61 for Australia, 64 for New Zealand, 44 for the United Kingdom. Calling Canada is the same as calling within the United States. Most local phone books list country codes and U.S. area codes. The country code for the United States is 1.

For operator assistance, dial "0." To obtain someone's phone number, call directory assistance, 555–1212 or occasionally 411 (free at public phones). To have the person you're calling foot the bill, phone collect; dial "0" instead of "1" before the 10-digit number.

At pay phones, instructions are usually posted. Generally you insert coins in a slot (10¢–35¢ for local calls) and wait for a steady tone before dialing. When you call long-distance, the operator tells you how much to insert; prepaid phone cards, widely available in various denominations, are easier. Call the number on the back, punch in the card's personal identification number when prompted, then dial your number.

Lei Greetings

When you walk off a long flight, perhaps a bit groggy and stiff, nothing quite compares with a Hawaiian lei greeting. The casual ceremony ranks as one of the fastest ways to make the transition from the worries of home to the joys of your vacation. Though the tradition has created an expectation that everyone receives this floral garland when they step off the plane, the state of Hawai'i cannot greet each of its nearly 7 million annual visitors.

Still, it's easy to **arrange for a lei ceremony for yourself or your companions before you arrive.** Contact one of the following companies if you have not signed up with a tour company that provides it. If you really want to be wowed by the experience, request a lei of tuberoses, some of the most divine-smelling blossoms on the planet. Aloha Lei Greeters charges $12 to $29 and needs at least one week's notice. Greeters of Hawai'i requires 48 hours' notice and charges $19.95 to $29.95 per person; add $10 for late notification. Kama'aina Ali'i, Flowers & Greeters charges $11.50 for a standard greeting on O'ahu.

➤**LEI GREETERS: Aloha Lei Greeters** (tel. 808/951–9990 or 800/367–5255, fax 808/951–9992). **Greeters of Hawai'i** (tel. 808/836–0161; 808/834–7667 for airport desk, fax 800/926–2644). **Kama'aina Ali'i, Flowers & Greeters** (tel. 808/836–3246 or 800/367–5183, fax 808/836–1814).

Lodging

The lodgings we list are the cream of the crop in each price category. We always list the facilities that are available, but we don't specify whether they cost extra. When pricing accommodations, always ask what's included and what costs extra.

Assume that hotels operate on the **European Plan** (EP, with no meals) unless we specify that they use the **Continental Plan** (CP, with a Continental breakfast), **Breakfast Plan** (BP, with a full breakfast), **Modified American Plan** (MAP, with breakfast and dinner), or the **Full American Plan** (FAP, with all meals).

CAMPING

Several national, state, and county parks are available, some with bathroom and cooking facilities, others a bit more primitive. The National Park Service and State Parks Division of the Hawai'i Department of Land and Natural Resources (☞ National and State Parks) can provide more information; details on local camping are available from the individual counties.

The City and County of Honolulu can provide information about camping at county sites on O'ahu; the State Parks Division, Hawai'i State Department of Land and Natural Resources handles the same questions for state camping sites. You can pack up your own sleeping bag and bring it along, or you can rent camping equipment at companies such as Omar the Tent Man on O'ahu.

➤**CAMPING AND RV FACILITIES: City and County of Honolulu** (tel. 808/523–4525). **State Parks Division, Hawai'i State Department of Land and Natural Resources** (tel. 808/587–0300). **Omar the Tent Man** (94-158 Leo'ole St., Waipahu, 96797, tel. 808/677–8785).

Money Matters

Many of the Islands' best attractions and activities, such as beaches and hiking, can be found in the form of natural beauty and cost nothing to view. You'll pay 50¢ for a daily newspaper, $1.50 to ride the bus anywhere on O'ahu, and from $45 on up to attend a lū'au. Large museums cost between $8 and $15 per entry; smaller ones can cost from $3 to $6. Prices throughout this guide are given for adults. Substantially reduced fees are almost always available for children, students, and senior citizens. For information on taxes, *see* Taxes.

ATMS

Automatic teller machines for easy access to cash are everywhere on the Islands. ATMs can be found in shopping centers, small convenience and grocery stores, inside hotels and resorts, as well as outside most bank branches. For a directory of locations, call 800/424–7787 for the MasterCard Cirrus Maestro network or 800/843–7587 for the Visa Plus network.

CREDIT CARDS

Most major credit cards are accepted throughout the Islands and are required to rent a car. When making reservations, double-check to ensure that the lodging, restaurant, or attraction you are planning to visit accepts them. In smaller concessions, B&Bs, and fast-food outlets, expect to pay cash.

Throughout this guide, the following abbreviations are used: **AE**, American Express; **D**, Discover; **DC**, Diners Club; **MC**, MasterCard; and **V**, Visa.

➤**REPORTING LOST CARDS: American Express** (tel. 800/528–4800). **Diners Club** (tel. 800/234–6377). **Discover** (tel. 800/347–2683). **MasterCard** (tel. 800/307–7309). **Visa** (tel. 800/847–2911).

Packing

Hawai'i is casual: sandals, bathing suits, and comfortable, informal clothing are the norm. In summer synthetic slacks and shirts, although easy to care for, can be uncomfortably warm. You'll easily find a bathing suit in Hawai'i, but **bring a bathing cap with you if you wear one.** You can waste hours searching for one.

Probably the most important thing to tuck into your suitcase is sunscreen. This is the tropics, and the ultraviolet rays are powerful. Consider using sunscreens with a sun protection factor (SPF) of 15 or higher. There are many tanning oils on the market in Hawai'i, including coconut and kukui (the nut from a local tree) oils, but they can cause severe burns. Hats and sunglasses offer important sun protection, too. All major hotels in Hawai'i provide beach towels.

As for clothing in the Hawaiian Islands, there's a saying that when a man wears a suit during the day, he's either going for a loan or he's a lawyer trying a case. Only a few upscale restaurants require a jacket for dinner. The aloha shirt is accepted dress in Hawai'i for business and most social occasions. Shorts are acceptable daytime attire, along with a T-shirt or polo shirt. Golfers should remember that many courses have dress codes requiring a collared shirt; call courses you're interested in for details. If you're visiting in winter or planning to visit a high-altitude area, **bring a sweater or light- to medium-weight jacket.**

To avoid customs and security delays, carry medications in their original packaging. **Don't pack any sharp objects in your carry-on luggage,** including knives of any size or material, scissors, manicure tools, and corkscrews, or anything else that might arouse suspicion.

Safety

Hawai'i is generally a safe tourist destination, but it's still wise to follow the same common sense safety precautions you would normally follow in your own hometown. Hotel and visitor center staff can provide information should you decide to head out on your own to more remote areas. Rental cars are magnets for break-ins, so **don't leave any valuables in the car**, not even in a locked trunk. **Avoid poorly lit areas, beach parks, and isolated areas after dark** as a precaution. When hiking, **stay on marked trails,** no matter how alluring the temptation might be to stray. Weather conditions can cause landscapes to become muddy, slippery, and tenuous, so staying on marked trails will lessen the possibility of a fall or getting lost. Ocean safety is of utmost importance when visiting an island destination. **Don't swim alone, and follow the international signage posted at beaches** that alerts swimmers to strong currents, man-of-war jellyfish, sharp coral, high surf, sharks, and dangerous shorebreaks. At coastal lookouts along cliff tops, heed the signs indicating that waves can climb over the ledges. Check with lifeguards at each beach for current conditions, and **if the red flags are up, indicating swimming and surfing are not allowed, don't go in.** Waters that look calm on the surface can harbor strong currents and undertows, and not a few people who were just wading have been dragged out to sea.

Sightseeing Tours

AERIAL TOURS

Through the bubble top of Honolulu Soaring Club's sleek sail plane you get aerial views of O'ahu's North Shore with its coral pools; sugarcane fields; windsurfers; and, in winter, humpback whales. On-board live videotaping is available. Reservations are not accepted; 20- and 30-minute flights leave every 20 minutes daily 10–5. The charge for one passenger is $90, two people fly for $120. Ask for "Mr. Bill" to make reservations.

Island Seaplane Service takes off from Keahi Lagoon and sets you soaring on an aerial tour that is either a half-hour South and Eastern O'ahu shoreline tour or an hour Circle Island tour. Get the feel of what Hawai'i air transportation was like during the Pan Am Clipper days for $89–$139.

Makani Kai Helicopters departs from Honolulu International Airport for helicopter tours of O'ahu by daylight or at sunset. A Waikīkī by Night excursion sends you soaring by the breathtaking Honolulu city lights. Tours range from $75 to $190, with customized tours available for $450.

➤**TOUR OPERATORS: Honolulu Soaring Club** (Dillingham Airfield, Mokulē'ia, tel. 808/677–3404). **Island Seaplane Service** (Keahi Lagoon, Honolulu, tel. 808/836–6273). **Makani Kai Helicopters** (Honolulu International Airport, Honolulu, tel. 808/834–5813, www.makanikai.com).

BOAT TOURS

Dream Cruises offers tours of Pearl Harbor aboard the 100-ft motor yacht *American Dream*. The trip takes place in the early morning—from 7:30 to 10:30—to coincide with the time that Pearl Harbor was attacked on December 7, 1941. It includes a stop near the *Arizona* Memorial, where the captain conducts a brief memorial service and lei placement ceremony. Narration and videos help describe the sights. In winter, this cruise is paired with a whale-watch. The cost is $21.95.

Tradewind Charters is a good bet for half-day private charter tours for sailing, snorkeling, and whale-watching. These luxury yachts not only eliminate crowds, but you also have the opportunity to "take the helm" if you wish. The cruise also includes snorkeling at an exclusive anchorage as well as hands-on snorkeling and sailing instruction. Charter prices are approximately $495 for up to six passengers.

➤**TOUR OPERATORS: Dream Cruises** (306 Kamani St., Honolulu, tel. 808/592–5200). **Tradewind Charters** (796 Kalanipuu St., Honolulu 96825, tel. 800/829–4899).

BUS AND VAN TOURS

There are many ground-tour companies in O'ahu that handle daylong sightseeing excursions. Depending on the size of the tour, travel may be by air-conditioned bus or smaller vans. Vans are recommended because less time is spent picking up passengers, and you get to know your fellow passengers and your tour guide. Ask exactly what the tour includes in the way of actual "get-off-the-bus" stops and "window sights." Most of the tour guides have taken special Hawaiiana classes to learn their history and lore, and many are certified by the state of Hawai'i. Tipping ($2 per person at least) is customary.

E Noa Tours uses minibuses and trolleys and likes to get you into the great outdoors. Polynesian Adventure Tours has motorcoaches, vans, and minicoaches. Polynesian Hospitality provides narrated tours. Roberts Hawai'i has equipment ranging from vans to presidential limousines. Trans Hawaiian Services offers multilingual tours.

Most tour companies offer some version of the following standard O'ahu tours listed below:

There are several variations on the Circle Island Tour theme. Some of these all-day tours, ranging from $45 to $65, include lunch. Little Circle tours cover East O'ahu. This is a half-day tour and costs between $25 and $40.

The comprehensive Pearl Harbor and City tour includes the boat tour to Pearl Harbor run by the National Park Service. These tours cost between $35 and $40.

One of the advantages of the Polynesian Cultural Center tour is that you don't have to drive yourself back to Waikīkī after dark if you take in the evening show. The tour is $70–$80 per person.

➤**TOUR OPERATORS: E Noa Tours** (tel. 808/591–9923, www. enoa.com). **Polynesian Adventure Tours** (tel. 808/833–3000, www.polyad.com). **Polynesian Cultural Center** (tel. 808/293–3333 or 808/923–1861, www.polynesia.com). **Polynesian Hospitality** (tel. 808/526–3565). **Roberts Hawai'i** (tel. 808/539–9400, www.robertshawaii.com). **Trans Hawaiian Services** (tel. 808/566–7300).

THEME TOURS

E Noa Tours has certified tour guides who conduct not only Circle Island and Pearl Harbor tours, but also shopping tours to the Waikele Premium Outlets.

Hawaiian Island Eco-Tours, Ltd.'s experienced guides take nature lovers and hikers on limited access trails for tours ranging from hidden waterfalls to birdwatching.

Home of the Brave offers military-history buffs a narrated tour of military bases plus a drive through the National Memorial Cemetery of the Pacific.

Mauka Makai Excursions takes visitors to visit some of the ancient Hawaiian archaeological, legendary, and nature sites that islanders hold sacred.

➤**TOUR OPERATORS: E Noa Tours** (tel. 808/591–9923, www. enoa.com). **Hawaiian Island Eco-tours, Ltd.** (tel. 808/236–7766, www.hikeoahu.com). **Home of the Brave** (tel. 808/396–8112). **Mauka Makai Excursions** (tel. 808/593–3525, www. hau-ecotours.com).

UNDERWATER TOURS

Atlantis Submarines operates two air-conditioned vessels off Waikīkī, which dive up to 100 ft for viewing of a sunken navy-yard oiler, coral gardens, and artificial reef teeming with tropical fish. Dive cruises are two hours in length, and are a popular family activity. Children must be at least 3 ft tall to board. Note: flash photography will not work; use film speed ASA 200 or above without flash. Tours cost $6 and begin from the Hilton Hawaiian Village Resort Pier.

➤**TOUR OPERATORS: *Atlantis Submarines*** (1600 Kapiʻolani Blvd., Suite 1630, Honolulu 96814, tel. 808/973–9800 or 800/548–6262, www.atlantisadventures.com).

WALKING TOURS

Meet at the Chinese Chamber of Commerce for a fascinating peek into herbal shops, an acupuncturist's office, open-air markets, and specialty stores. The 2½-hour tour sponsored by the Chinese Chamber of Commerce costs $5 and is available every Tuesday at 9:30. Reservations are required.

The Mission Houses Museum offers a two-hour walk through historic Honolulu that begins with an hour-long tour of the Mission Houses before the downtown stroll. Reservations are required. Tours are $8 and operate Thursday and Friday mornings beginning at 10.

The American Institute of Architects offers a tour of downtown Honolulu from an architectural perspective. Tours cost $15 per person and run Tuesday and Saturday mornings at 9:30.

The Hawaii Geographic Society offers a unique downtown Honolulu historic temple and archaeology walking tour (Sunday only upon request) for $10 per person.

History springs to life for young and old alike during Honolulu Time Walks, which come with appropriately costumed narrators and cost $7–$45. Tours and seminar programs explore the "mysteries" of Honolulu—its haunts, historic neighborhoods, and the different but not always talked about eras in its colorful history.

➤**TOUR OPERATORS: AIA Downtown Walking Tour** (American Institute of Architects, 1128 Nuʻuanu Ave., Honolulu, tel. 808/545–4242). **Chinatown Walking Tour** (Chinese Chamber of

Commerce, 42 N. King St., Honolulu, tel. 808/533–3181). **Historic Downtown Walking Tour** (553 S. King St., Honolulu, tel. 808/531–0481). **Hawaii Geographic Society** (tel. 808/538–3952). **Honolulu Time Walks** (2634 S. King St., Suite 3, Honolulu, tel. 808/943–0371).

Taxes

There is a 4.16% state sales tax on all purchases, including food. A hotel room tax of 7.25%, combined with the sales tax of 4%, equals an 11.25% rate added onto your hotel bill. A $2-per-day road tax is also assessed on each rental vehicle.

Taxis

You can usually get a taxi right outside your hotel. Most restaurants will call a taxi for you. Rates are $1.50 at the drop of the flag, plus $1.50 per mile. Drivers are generally courteous, and the cars are in good condition, many of them air-conditioned. For transportation throughout the island, try Charley's Taxi & Tours. SIDA of Hawai'i Taxis, Inc. offers 24-hour islandwide transportation service and multilingual drivers.

➤**TAXI COMPANIES: Charley's Taxi & Tours** (tel. 808/531–1333). **SIDA of Hawai'i Taxis Inc.** (tel. 808/836–0011).

Time

Hawai'i is on Hawaiian Standard Time, 5 hours behind New York, 2 hours behind Los Angeles, and 10 hours behind London.

When the U.S. mainland is on daylight saving time, Hawai'i is not, so add an extra hour of time difference between the Islands and U.S. mainland destinations. You may also find that things generally move more slowly here. That has nothing to do with your watch—it's just the laid-back way called Hawaiian time.

Tipping

Tip cab drivers 15% of the fare. Standard tips for restaurants and bar tabs runs from 15% to 20% of the bill, depending on the standard of service. Bellhops at hotels usually receive $1 per bag, more if you have bulky items such as bicycles and surfboards. Tip the hotel-room maid $1 per night, paid daily. Tip doormen $1 for assistance with taxis; tips for concierge vary depending on the service. For example, tip more for "hard-to-get" event tickets or dining reservations.

Tours & Packages

Packages that include any combination of lodging, airfare, meals, sightseeing, car rental, and even sports activities and entertainment are popular in Hawai'i and are often considerably cheaper than piecing the vacation together à la carte. Just do your research, and make sure that the options offered (especially when it comes to lodging and meals) are really the ones you want.

BOOKING WITH AN AGENT

Travel agents are excellent resources. But it's a good idea to collect brochures from several agencies, as some agents' suggestions may be influenced by relationships with tour and package firms that reward them for volume sales. If you have a special interest, **find an agent with expertise in that area**; the American Society of Travel Agents (ASTA; ☞ Travel Agencies) has a database of specialists worldwide.

Make sure your travel agent knows the accommodations and other services of the place being recommended. Ask about the hotel's location, room size, beds, and whether it has a pool, room service, or programs for children, if you care about these. Has your agent been there in person or sent others whom you can contact?

Do some homework on your own, too: local tourism boards can provide information about lesser-known and small-niche operators, some of which may sell only direct.

BUYER BEWARE

Each year consumers are stranded or lose their money when tour operators—even large ones with excellent reputations—go out of business. So check out the operator. Ask several travel agents about its reputation, and try to **book with a company that has a consumer-protection program.** (Look for information in the company's brochure.) In the United States, members of the National Tour Association and the United States Tour Operators Association are required to set aside funds to cover your payments and travel arrangements in the event that the company defaults. It's also a good idea to choose a company that participates in the American Society of Travel Agents' Tour Operator Program (TOP); ASTA will act as mediator in any disputes between you and your tour operator.

Remember that the more your package or tour includes the better you can predict the ultimate cost of your vacation. Make sure you know exactly what is covered, and **beware of hidden costs.** Are taxes, tips, and transfers included? Entertainment and excursions? These can add up.

➤ **TOUR-OPERATOR RECOMMENDATIONS: American Society of Travel Agents** (☞ Travel Agencies). **National Tour Association** (NTA; 546 E. Main St., Lexington, KY 40508, tel. 859/226–4444 or 800/682–8886, www.ntaonline.com). **United States Tour Operators Association** (USTOA; 275 Madison Ave., Suite 2014, New York, NY 10016, tel. 212/599–6599 or 800/468–7862, fax 212/599–6744, www.ustoa.com).

Trolley Travel

The Waikīkī Trolley has three lines and 40 stops that allow you to design your own itinerary. The Red Line cruises around Waikīkī,

Ala Moana, and downtown Honolulu. The Yellow Line hits major shopping centers and restaurant locations. The Blue Line provides a tour of O'ahu's southeastern coastline, including Hanauma Bay and Sea Life Park. The trolleys depart from the Royal Hawaiian Shopping Center in Waikīkī every 15 minutes daily from 8 to 4:30. Buy an all-day pass from the conductor for $18. The Rainbow Trolley System picks up riders at the Waikīkī Beachcomber Hotel every 30 minutes and tours "outer Waikīkī" with trolley routes through Kaimuki, Ala Moana shopping district, and Downtown Honolulu.

➤CONTACTS: **Rainbow Trolley** (tel. 808/539–9400). **Waikīkī Trolley** (tel. 808/593–2822, www.waikikitrolley.com).

Travel Agencies

A good travel agent puts your needs first. Look for an agency that has been in business at least five years, emphasizes customer service, and has someone on staff who specializes in your destination. In addition, **make sure the agency belongs to a professional trade organization.** The American Society of Travel Agents (ASTA)—the largest and most influential in the field with more than 24,000 members in some 140 countries—maintains and enforces a strict code of ethics and will step in to help mediate any agent-client dispute involving ASTA members if necessary. ASTA (whose motto is "Without a travel agent, you're on your own") also maintains a Web site that includes a directory of agents. (If a travel agency is also acting as your tour operator, *see* Buyer Beware in Tours & Packages.)

➤LOCAL AGENT REFERRALS: **American Society of Travel Agents** (ASTA; 1101 King St., Suite 200, Alexandria, VA 22314, tel. 800/965–2782 24-hr hot line, fax 703/739–3268, www.astanet. com). **Association of British Travel Agents** (68–71 Newman St., London W1T 3AH, tel. 020/7637–2444, fax 020/7637–0713, www.abtanet.com). **Association of Canadian Travel Agents** (130 Albert St., Suite 1705, Ottawa, Ontario K1P 5G4, tel.

613/237–3657, fax 613/237–7052, www.acta.net). **Australian Federation of Travel Agents** (Level 3, 309 Pitt St., Sydney, NSW 2000, tel. 02/9264–3299, fax 02/9264–1085, www.afta.com.au). **Travel Agents' Association of New Zealand** (Level 5, Tourism and Travel House, 79 Boulcott St., Box 1888, Wellington 10033, tel. 04/499–0104, fax 04/499–0827, www.taanz.org.nz).

Visitor Information

Before you go, contact the Hawai'i Visitors & Convention Bureau for general information on each island, free brochures that include an accommodations and car-rental guide, and an entertainment and dining listing containing one-line descriptions of bureau members.

➤**TOURIST INFORMATION: Hawai'i Attractions Association** (tel. 808/596–7733, www.hawaiiattractions.com). **Hawai'i Visitors & Convention Bureau** (Waikīkī Business Plaza, 2270 Kalākaua Ave., Suite 801, Honolulu 96815, tel. 808/923–1811 or 800/464–2924, www.gohawaii.com). **O'ahu Visitor Bureau** (tel. 877/525–6248, www.visit-oahu.com). **Surf Report** (tel. 808/973–4383). **Weather** (tel. 808/973–4381).

Web Sites

For more information on Hawai'i, visit www.gohawaii.com, the official Web site of the Hawai'i Visitors and Convention Bureau.

Other sites to check out include www.visit-Oahu.com (O'ahu Visitors Bureau); www.alohaboatdays.com (for a schedule and information about cruise-arrival celebrations at Aloha Tower, Honolulu Harbor); and www.honoluluweekly.com for a weekly guide to the arts, entertainment, and dining in Honolulu.

When to Go

Long days of sunshine and fairly mild year-round temperatures make Hawai'i an all-season destination. Most resort areas are at sea level, with average afternoon temperature during the coldest winter months of December and January at 75°F; during the hottest months of August and September the temperature often reaches 92°F.

Most travelers head to the Islands during winter. From mid-December through mid-April, visitors from the mainland and other areas covered with snow find Hawai'i's sun-splashed beaches and balmy trade winds appealing. This high season means that fewer travel bargains are available; room rates average 10%–15% higher during this season than the rest of the year.

Rainfall can be high in winter, particularly on the north and east shores of each island. Generally speaking, you are guaranteed sun and warm temperatures on the west and south shores no matter what time of year.

CLIMATE

The following are average maximum and minimum temperatures for Honolulu; the temperatures throughout the Hawaiian Islands are similar.

➤FORECASTS: **Weather Channel Connection** (tel. 900/932–8437), 95¢ per minute from a Touch-Tone phone.

HONOLULU, O'AHU

Jan.	80F	27C	May	85F	29C	Sept.	88F	31C
	65	18		70	21		73	23
Feb.	80F	27C	June	86F	30C	Oct.	87F	31C
	65	18		72	22		72	22
Mar.	81F	27C	July	87F	31C	Nov.	84F	29C
	69	21		73	23		69	21
Apr.	83F	28C	Aug.	88F	31C	Dec.	81F	27C
	69	21		74	23		67	19

index

Fodor's
Key to the Guides

America's guidebook leader publishes guides for every kind of traveler. Check out our many series and find your perfect match.

Fodor's Gold Guides

America's favorite travel-guide series offers the most detailed insider reviews of hotels, restaurants, and attractions in all price ranges, plus great background information, smart tips, and useful maps.

Fodor's Road Guide USA

Big guides for a big country—the most comprehensive guides to America's roads, packed with places to stay, eat, and play across the U.S.A. Just right for road warriors, family vacationers, and cross-country trekkers.

COMPASS AMERICAN GUIDES

Stunning guides from top local writers and photographers, with gorgeous photos, literary excerpts, and colorful anecdotes. A must-have for culture mavens, history buffs, and new residents.

Fodor's CITYPACKS

Concise city coverage with a foldout map. The right choice for urban travelers who want everything under one cover.

Fodor's EXPLORING GUIDES

Hundreds of color photos bring your destination to life. Lively stories lend insight into the culture, history, and people.

Fodor's POCKET GUIDES

For travelers who need only the essentials. The best of Fodor's in pocket-size packages for just $9.95.

Fodor's To Go
Credit-card–size, magnetized color microguides that fit in the palm of your hand—perfect for "stealth" travelers or as gifts.

Fodor's FLASHMAPS
Every resident's map guide. 60 easy-to-follow maps of public transit, parks, museums, zip codes, and more.

Fodor's CITYGUIDES
Sourcebooks for living in the city: Thousands of in-the-know listings for restaurants, shops, sports, nightlife, and other city resources.

Fodor's AROUND THE CITY WITH KIDS
68 great ideas for family days, recommended by resident parents. Perfect for exploring in your own backyard or on the road.

Fodor's ESCAPES
Fill your trip with once-in-a-lifetime experiences, from ballooning in Chianti to overnighting in the Moroccan desert. These full-color dream books point the way.

Fodor's FYI
Get tips from the pros on planning the perfect trip. Learn how to pack, fly hassle-free, plan a honeymoon or cruise, stay healthy on the road, and travel with your baby.

Fodor's Languages for Travelers
Practice the local language before hitting the road. Available in phrase books, cassette sets, and CD sets.

Karen Brown's Guides
Engaging guides to the most charming inns and B&Bs in the U.S.A. and Europe, with easy-to-follow inn-to-inn itineraries.

Baedeker's Guides
Comprehensive guides, trusted since 1829, packed with A–Z reviews and star ratings.

At bookstores everywhere.   www.fodors.com/books

FODOR'S POCKET HONOLULU AND WAIKĪKĪ

EDITOR: Carissa Bluestone

Editorial Contributors: Daniel Taras, Maggie Wunsch

Editorial Production: Ira-Neil Dittersdorf, Taryn Luciani

Maps: David Lindroth, *cartographer;* Bob Blake and Rebecca Baer, *map editors*

Design: Fabrizio La Rocca, *creative director;* Tigist Getachew, *art director;* Jolie Novak, *senior picture editor*

Production/Manufacturing: Angela L. McLean

Cover Photo (O'ahu): Macduff Everton/Corbis

IMPORTANT TIP

Although all prices, opening times, and other details in this book are based on information supplied to us at press time, changes occur all the time in the travel world, and Fodor's cannot accept responsibility for facts that become outdated or for inadvertent errors or omissions. So always confirm information when it matters, especially if you're making a detour to visit a specific place.

SPECIAL SALES

Fodor's Travel Publications are available at special discounts for bulk purchases for sales promotions or premiums. Special editions, including personalized covers, excerpts of existing guides, and corporate imprints, can be created in large quantities for special needs. For more information, contact your local bookseller or write to Special Markets, Fodor's Travel Publications, 1745 Broadway, New York, NY, 10019. Inquiries from Canada should be directed to your local Canadian bookseller or sent to Random House of Canada, Ltd., Marketing Department, 2775 Matheson Boulevard East, Mississauga, Ontario L4W 4P7. Inquiries from the United Kingdom should be sent to Fodor's Travel Publications, 20 Vauxhall Bridge Road, London SW1V 2SA, England.

PRINTED IN THE UNITED STATES OF AMERICA

10 9 8 7 6 5 4 3 2 1